WHAT WOULD YOU DO?

A Kid's Guide to Dealing with Tricky and Sticky Situations

What Would You Do?
A Kid's Guide to Dealing with Tricky and Sticky Situations
Copyright © 1990 by Linda Schwartz
Written by Linda Schwartz
Illustrated by Beverly Armstrong

Revised Edition © 2018 Creative Teaching Press Inc.
Illustrator: Gloria Y. Jenkins
Editor: Jasmine Tabrizi
Designer: Tawney Johnson
Art Director: Moonhee Pak
Project Director: Stacey Faulkner

DEDICATION

This book is dedicated to Michael and Stephen and
to all the kids who meet the unexpected
on the path to growing up.

ACKNOWLEDGMENTS

Sincere thanks to the following group of special people for sharing their knowledge and expertise: Michael Espino, director of health and safety services for the Santa Barbara County chapter of the American Red Cross; Arlene Radasky, chairman of youth services for the Santa Barbara County chapter of the American Red Cross; Ben Gonzalez, police juvenile detective; Dennis Naiman, principal of La Patera Elementary School; and Sue Perona, fifth-grade teacher at Mountain View Elementary School.

CONTENTS >>>

111

FIRST AID SITUATIONS

165

**LISTS AND
CHECKLISTS**

A NOTE TO KIDS

Your challenge is to cope with these situations—to think them through and decide what you would do.

>>> Life is full of surprises. Some of these surprises are pleasant, like opening a birthday gift or having a favorite relative stop by for a visit. Some of these surprises are unpleasant, like waking up with the chicken pox or finding a flat tire on your bike. And some of these surprises are downright scary, like hearing noises outside a window when you are home alone or waking up to the smell of smoke.

Illness, flat tires, prowlers, and fires are only a few of the tricky and sticky situations you'll read about in **What Would You Do?** The author of this book describes more than 70 different situations you might encounter at home, at or on the way to school, when you are out and about, or in an emergency.

These situations vary in seriousness. Some of them are merely awkward or embarrassing.

Some of them are frightening or dangerous. And some of them are life-threatening. The purpose of this book is to help you plan for these situations in advance so that you will be better prepared to deal with them if and when they arise.

Your challenge is to cope with these situations—to think them through and decide what you would do. First, select and read about one of these situations. Next, before you turn the page, think about what you would do if you found yourself in this situation.

Then, turn the page and read the steps that are listed. Ask yourself if these steps are the same as those you thought of. Did you have some additional ideas? Finally, talk over these steps—both the ones listed in the book and the ones you thought of—with other members of your family. Modify the steps that are listed to meet your needs, and discuss additional steps you might take in a similar situation.

If you are prepared in advance, you'll be able to act quickly, and you'll feel more confident because you'll know that what you decide to do is right. By doing the right thing, you may be able to make an awkward situation less embarrassing and to prevent a serious situation from becoming a life-threatening one.

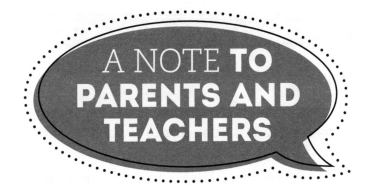

A NOTE **TO** PARENTS AND TEACHERS

The purpose of **What Would You Do?** is to provide some of that guidance in advance.

In the course of growing up, most children encounter a variety of unexpected situations when they are at home, when they are at school, and when they are out and about. If children are alone in these situations, they must decide what to do with little or no on-the-spot guidance from parents, teachers, or other adults.

The purpose of **What Would You Do?** is to provide some of that guidance in advance. This book is designed to help children think about and plan for tricky and sticky situations beforehand so that they will be better prepared to deal with these situations when they arise. It provides children with a list of steps they can follow in caring safely for themselves and others until help comes.

Of course, no book can be all things to all children because no one can imagine all possible situations, anticipate all probable reactions, and/or describe all practicable solutions. For these reasons, **What Would You Do?** is intended to be used as a guide, not as a manual. It suggests a direction to take but does not prescribe all of the steps that should be followed in getting there.

Encourage the children in your care to select and read one of the situation descriptions and—before turning the page—to think about what actions they would take if they found themselves in that situation. Suggest that they put their actions in order so that they will do the most important things first.

Once the children have decided what they would do, tell them to turn the page and check their ideas against the steps that are listed. Help them compare their ideas with those in the book. Talk about specific similarities and differences and the reasons for them. Modify the steps that are listed in any way necessary to make them pertain to your specific family or classroom situation and match the maturity levels and abilities of your children.

The situations described in this book make ideal topics for discussion or units for study. Situation descriptions can be used to spark dinner table conversation, to pass idle hours while traveling, to replace television programs and video games as a source of entertainment, or to fill the final restless moments before the bell rings at school.

Several situation descriptions can be combined to create special study units. For example, one or more of the fire situations (see pages 39-44) might be used as part of a unit for Fire Prevention Week. In conjunction with this unit, children might be encouraged to check their homes or classrooms for fire hazards, to plan and practice fire escape routes, to make posters urging fire safety, and to visit a local fire station. Similarly, the situations on other pages might

be combined to create units on topics ranging from Dangerous Strangers to Natural Disasters.

In group settings, these situations can be used for role playing and for cooperative learning. For example, parts can be assigned and children can create their own dialogue.

In addition to descriptions of more than 70 situations, this book also contains seven lists and checklists, a glossary, an index, and diagrams that show how to find a heartbeat, stop bleeding, aid a person who is choking, and shut off the flow of natural gas and water.

Children who have thought about a situation in advance will be able to react more quickly in that situation because they'll know what is expected of them and what they should do. By doing the right thing in a crisis, they may be able to prevent a sticky situation from becoming serious, to protect themselves from danger, or to even save a life.

In this section, you will find descriptions of situations you might encounter in your home. Among these situations are

blackouts, broken water pipes, electrical fires, cyberbullying, prowlers, and sick pets.

First, read about the situation. Next, think about what you would do if you found yourself in this situation. Then, turn the page and read the steps that are listed. Finally, talk over these steps with other members of your family and discuss additional steps you might take in a similar situation.

LOCKED OUT!

Returning home from school, you realize that you have lost your key. You are locked out, and no one else is home.

- Stay with a friend until a family member comes home and can unlock the door and let you in.

- Call your parents at work and tell them where you are.

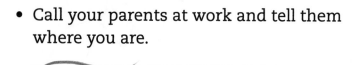

- To avoid being locked out again, hide an extra key in a secret place that only members of your family know about.

- If you cannot safely hide a key, leave an extra one with a neighbor you trust.

BREAK-IN

When you come home from school, you notice that the door is open. You know that no one else is supposed to be home at this hour. You suspect that someone has broken in.

- Do not go inside. The person who broke in may still be there.

- Instead, go to a neighbor and tell him or her what you saw.

- Dial 911 or call the police or sheriff's department.

- While help is on the way, notice any unfamiliar vehicles that are parked nearby. Write down their descriptions and the numbers and letters that appear on their license plates.

Red pickup truck
549 SMJ

White Toyota
station wagon
AUB 028

Small yellow Honda
2 AJX III

Gray Ford sedan
1 BGL 044

all California plates

STRANGER AT **THE DOOR**

You are home alone. You hear a knock.

You look out and see someone you do not

know—a stranger—standing at your door.

- Do not open the door. Leave it closed and locked.

- To let the stranger know someone is home, ask "Who's there?" or "Who is it?"

- Do not tell the stranger anything. Do not say that you are home alone or mention when your parents plan to return. Instead, say only that your parents can't come to the door.

- If the stranger does not leave right away or you feel uncomfortable with the situation for any reason, call a neighbor, report the incident to the police or sheriff's department, or dial 911.

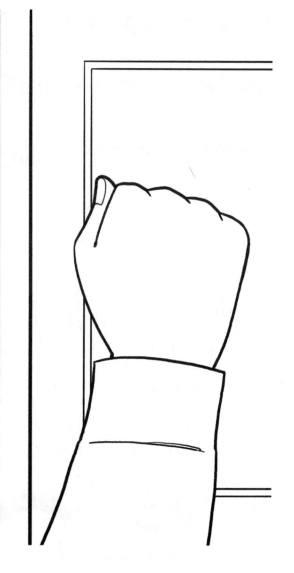

PROWLER

It's nighttime. You are babysitting your younger sister. She is sleeping, and you are reading in bed. You think you hear someone outside the bedroom window.

- Go to a telephone and call the police or sheriff's department or dial 911.

- Turn on a radio or a television set and inside lights.

- Check all doors and windows to make sure that they are securely locked, starting with the ground floor.

- Close all blinds, curtains, and drapes, and pull down the shades.

- Turn on all outdoor lights if you can do so safely using indoor switches. **Do not** go outside.

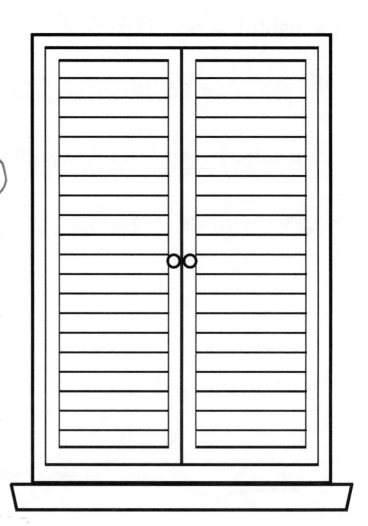

SICK **PET**

One afternoon when you come home, your dog does not greet you at the door. You find her lying in a corner. She has thrown up on the kitchen floor and appears to be sick. No one else is home, and your parents aren't answering their phones.

- Look around for something your dog has gotten into that might have made her sick.

- If you find spoiled food, a household cleanser, a pesticide, pills, or anything else that might be poisonous, call your veterinarian. Describe the substance and the dog's symptoms, and ask what you should do.

- If you cannot find any evidence of poisoning, the dog may simply be suffering from an upset stomach. One of the best treatments for this ailment is letting the stomach rest. Do not give the dog anything to eat. Pick up the dog's food dish and place it out of reach.

- Make fresh water available for the dog, but do not try to make her drink.

- Clean up the mess on the kitchen floor.

- Call your parents to let them know what has happened.

WATER

PERSONAL **ILLNESS**

On the way home from school, you begin to

feel sick. Your whole body aches, and your

head is very warm. Every step is an effort.

When you reach the door, you are glad to be

home—but you wish you weren't home alone.

- Call a parent to let him or her know that you are not feeling well. Tell your parent what hurts, and ask what you should do.

- Do not take any medicine unless your parent tells you to do so.

- Drink water, fruit juices, or light-colored soft drinks.

- Get into bed, relax, and try to sleep.

ANSWERING THE PHONE

You are home alone. The telephone rings. You answer, and a person

whose voice you do not recognize asks if your mother is home.

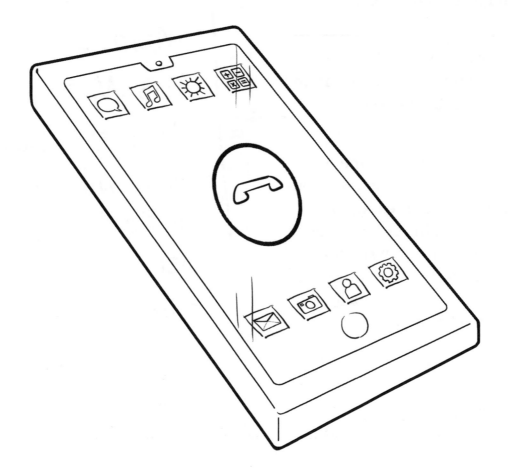

- Do not let the caller know that you are home alone.

- Tell the caller that your mother can't come to the phone right now but that you would be glad to take a message.

- Always keep a small pad of paper and a pencil or pen in a central location to make message taking easier.

- Write down the day and time of the call, the caller's name and telephone number, and a brief message. Ask the caller to spell his or her name if you aren't sure how to write it and to repeat any part of the number or message that you may have misunderstood or missed.

Sunday,
10/28
12:30 PM

Mom —
Mrs. Wilson said that the bake sale will be next Saturday. I told her we'd bring cupcakes.

Brian

CYBERBULLYING

Just as you are about to shut down your device, you receive a message. You read it. The person who sent the message uses mean words and makes aggressive threats.

- Turn the device off right away.

- Do not respond.

- Do not delete the message. Keep it as evidence to help identify the bully.

- Tell an adult about the message.

- If you continue to receive these kinds of messages, block the person to avoid any more harassment.

- Report the bullying to the cellular or Internet service provider.

- Report serious bullying, such as physical or sexual threats, to the police.

BLACKOUT

Your parents have gone out for the evening, and your best friend is spending the night with you. All of a sudden, the electricity goes off. The room is completely dark.

- If the lights are out only in one part of your house, the problem is probably a blown fuse or tripped circuit breaker.

- Stay in the lighted part of your house.

- Do not try to change the fuse or reset the circuit breaker. Let your parents do that when they come home.

- If the lights are out in every room in your house and in every house on your block, the problem is probably a power outage, or blackout.

- Wait a few minutes. In most instances of blackout, power is restored quickly.

- If the power does not come back on within a few minutes, find and turn on a flashlight. You should keep flashlights handy in several parts of your house for use in emergencies. Do not light candles or matches.

- Avoid using stairs in the dark.

- Make a list of at least five things you could do safely for fun during a blackout.

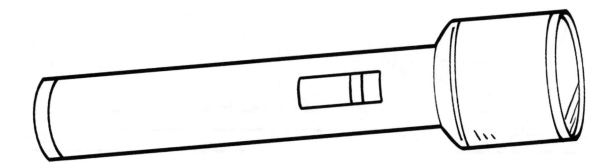

BROKEN **WATER PIPE**

You are home alone. You get thirsty. You go to the kitchen for a

drink. The kitchen floor is wet. You think a water pipe has broken.

- Do not touch a light switch or turn on any electrical appliance while you are standing on the wet kitchen floor. If the room is dark, use a flashlight.

- Call your parents to tell them about the break. If they don't answer, follow the steps below.

- Look under the sink to see if you can find the break.

- Locate the water shutoff wheel that is attached to the pipe under the sink.

- If the pipe break is **above** this wheel, turn the wheel to the right (clockwise) until the water stops flowing. See diagram on page 175.

- If the pipe break is **below** this wheel, call the apartment manager or ask a neighbor to help you turn off the water.

- Roll up cloth towels and lay them in kitchen doorways to soak up the water and keep it from reaching carpets, rugs, or wood floors.

- Use a mop or sponge and a bucket to wipe up the water.

- Avoid using the effected faucets until your parents have had a plumber repair or replace the pipe.

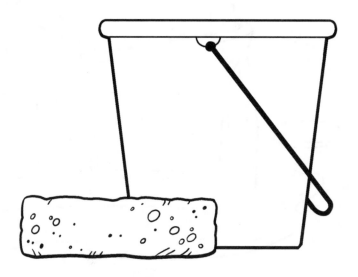

NATURAL GAS LEAK

You are home alone after school. Feeling hungry, you go into the kitchen to get a snack. You smell gas and think it must be coming from the stove. When you check the knobs, you discover that all of them are in the **off** position. The only possible explanation for the odor is a natural gas leak.

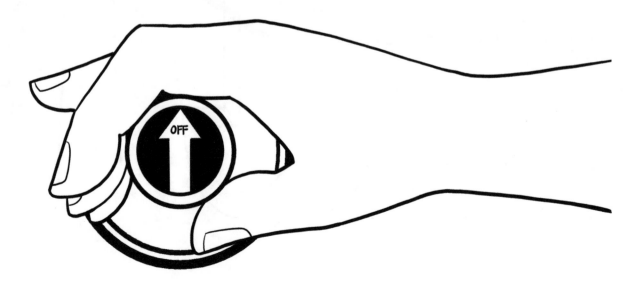

- Do not flip an electrical switch or light a match. Doing either one could ignite trapped gas, causing an explosion and fire.

- Open a kitchen window so that fresh air can come in and reduce the concentration of gas.

- Get out of the kitchen, and close the door behind you.

- Call the gas company to report the leak.

- Get in touch with your parents to tell them about the leak.

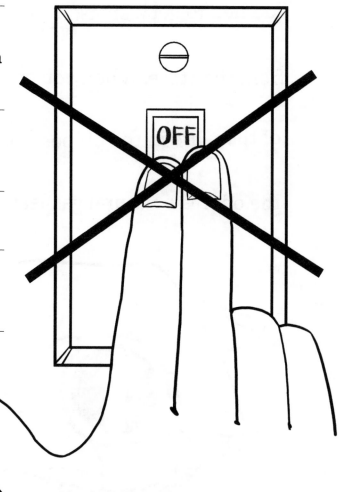

ELECTRICAL **FIRE**

While you are toasting bread for a sandwich,

a shower of blue sparks and thick smoke

comes from the electrical outlet.

- Turn off the toaster.

- Unplug the toaster if you can do so safely.

- Use a fire extinguisher. If one is not handy, use baking soda. Never use water on an electrical fire. Electricity travels through water, so throwing water on the fire can make it larger and give you an electrical shock.

- Get out of the kitchen, and close the door behind you.

- Dial 911 or call the operator or fire department.

- Even though you are anxious, take time to speak clearly and remember to give your address so the firefighters can find the fire!

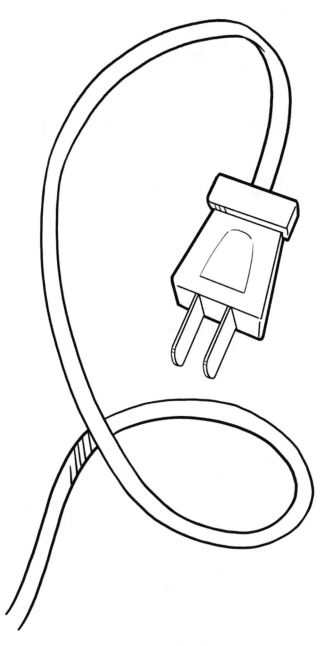

HOUSE FIRE

During the night, you wake up coughing.

Your eyes burn. You smell smoke. You call out,

but no one answers. Everyone else is asleep.

- Shout loudly to wake up others.

- If your bedroom door is closed, feel it with your hand. If it is hot, do not open it.

- If your bedroom door is open, and you can feel heat or see flames, do not walk toward the fire. Instead, close the door.

- If you are on the ground floor, exit through a window.

- If you are not on the ground floor, stay in your room and wait for help.

- Place sheets, towels, or clothes along the bottom of the door to keep smoke from coming in.

- If there is a phone in your room, dial 911 or call the operator or fire department.

- Stay by the window so firefighters can find you quickly.

- If your door does not feel hot and you do not see flames, leave.

- If there is a lot of smoke, tie a handkerchief, scarf, or T-shirt over your nose and mouth. Then crawl to the nearest exit.

- Once you are safely outside, go to your family's designated meeting spot. Send someone to call 911 or the fire department.

FIRE NEXT DOOR

You are home alone. You hear popping sounds and smell smoke. Curious, you look out your bedroom window to see what is happening. You discover that smoke and flames are pouring from the house next door.

- Dial 911 or call the operator or fire department and report the fire. Be sure to give the address of the house that is burning. If you aren't sure what it is, give your own address. Once the firefighters are on the right street and in the right block, they will be able to see which house the flames are coming from.

- Alert your neighbors by phone if you know their telephone number.

- Once the firefighters arrive, tell them what you know about how many family members there are, who works when, who sleeps where, and whether or not people or pets might be trapped inside.

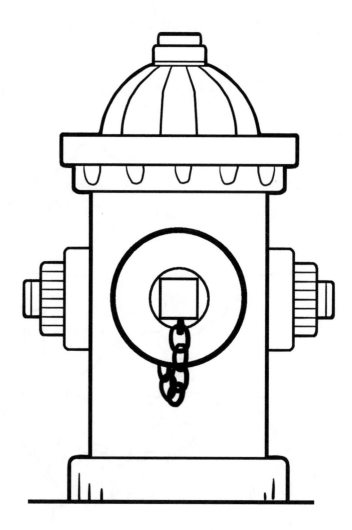

SEXUAL **ABUSE**

You are home alone. A family friend comes over for a visit.

Because you recognize him, you invite him to come in. While

talking to you, he begins touching a private part of your body.

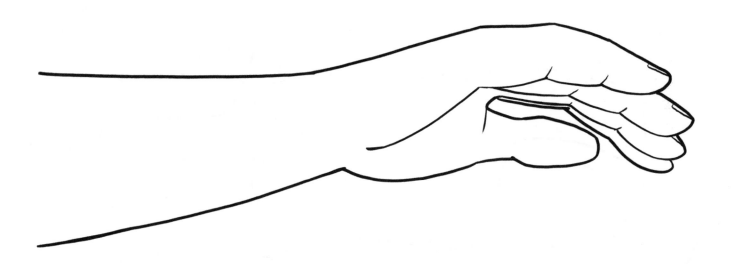

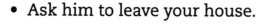

- Tell him firmly to remove his hands from your body.

  _____

- Ask him to leave your house.

  _____

- When your parents come home, tell them what happened.

  _____

- Never again allow this person to come in when you are home alone.

  _____

In this section, you will find descriptions of situations you might encounter while you are at school or while you are traveling to and from school. Among these situations are

| bullies, | flat tires, | forgotten lunches, |
| pills on the playground, | stolen property, | and friendly strangers. |

First, read about the situation. Next, think about what you would do if you found yourself in this situation. Then, turn the page and read the steps that are listed. Finally, talk over these steps with other members of your family and discuss additional steps you might take in a similar situation.

BROKEN GLASS

On the way to school, you trip and fall. Luckily, you are not hurt, but the two glass jars you had planned to use for your science experiment now lie shattered on the sidewalk.

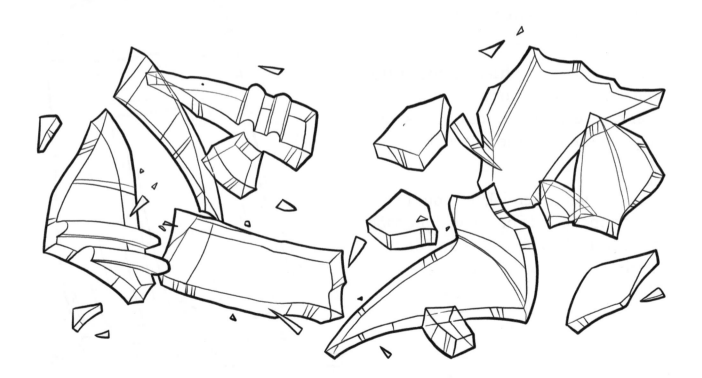

- Carefully pick up the large pieces of glass and place them where other walkers are not likely to step or fall on them.

- If you are near a friend's house, knock on the door and ask to borrow a dustpan and broom. Sweep the broken glass into the dustpan and then empty the dustpan into a wastebasket or garbage can.

- If you are not near a friend's house, use a sheet of cardboard or a folded piece of paper to sweep the shards of glass together and push them off the sidewalk.

- When you get to school, tell your teacher what happened. He or she will probably let you bring two more jars and do the experiment on another day.

FLAT **TIRE**

While you are riding to school on your bike, one of your tires goes flat. You are only three blocks away from school, but your house is ten blocks away, and you don't want to be late for class.

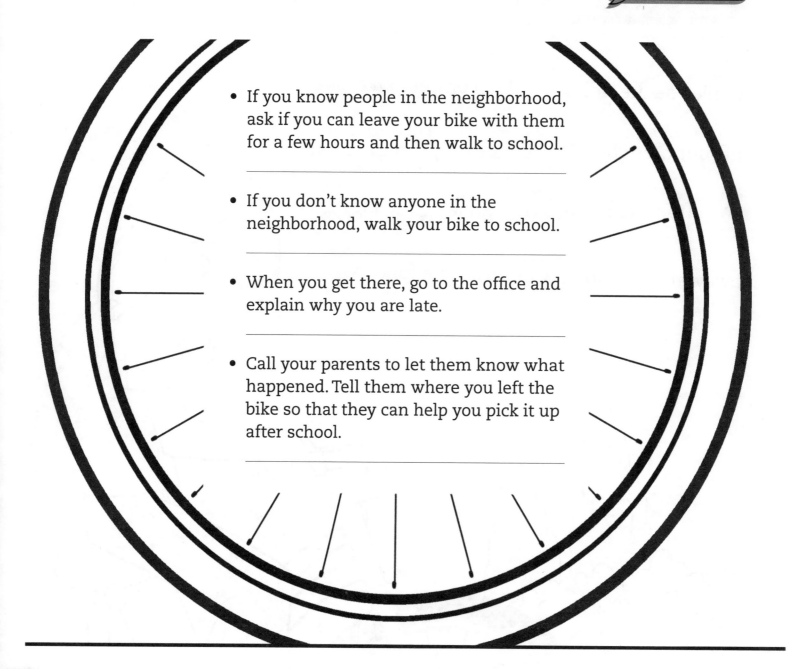

- If you know people in the neighborhood, ask if you can leave your bike with them for a few hours and then walk to school.

- If you don't know anyone in the neighborhood, walk your bike to school.

- When you get there, go to the office and explain why you are late.

- Call your parents to let them know what happened. Tell them where you left the bike so that they can help you pick it up after school.

BURGLARY IN PROGRESS

One morning on your way to school, you notice two strangers standing near your neighbors' window. You know that your neighbors are on vacation. You think that the strangers may be trying to break in.

BURGLARY IN PROGRESS

- Do not confront the strangers.

- If you have a cell phone, call your mom or dad and tell them what you saw. If your parents do not answer, call 911 and report the incident.

- If you don't have a phone but are near home, go back and tell your mom or dad what you saw. If your parents are not home, call the police or sheriff's department and report the incident.

- If you are far from home but you are near a friend's place, go there and tell an adult what you saw.

- If you are not near home and do not know anyone along the way, go straight to school. As soon as you get there, report the incident to your teacher, school secretary, or principal.

SUSPICIOUS **DRIVER**

As you are walking to school, a car pulls alongside you. In a friendly voice, the driver asks how to find a particular street, building, or address. When you do not answer, he becomes upset. In a gruff voice, he tells you to get in the car and help him find it.

- If a driver starts following you or asks you a question, do not stop walking. Keep moving and stay as far away from the car as possible.

- If the suspicious driver goes away, write down the numbers and letters on his license plate and the kind and color of his car. As soon as you get to school, describe the incident and give this information to your teacher, the school secretary, or the principal.

- If the suspicious driver continues to follow you, go to the nearest house where there are signs that someone is home. Explain to the first adult you see that you are being followed and ask if you can come inside to call the police.

STOVE **LEFT ON**

While sitting in class, you suddenly remember that you left

home without turning off the stove. You go to the office and

call home, but no one answers the phone.

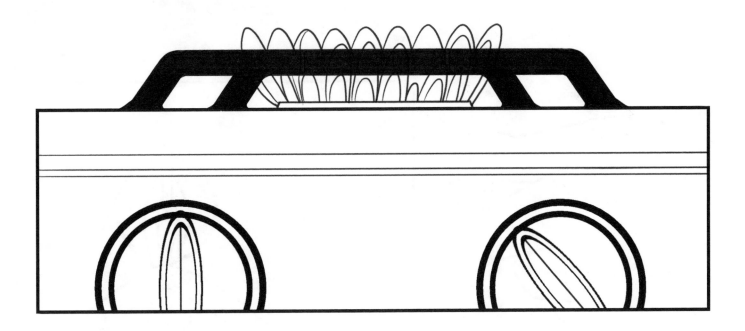

STOVE LEFT ON

- If your neighbor has a key to your door, call and ask him or her to go into your house and turn off the stove.

- Ask a relative who has a key to turn off the stove.

- Have the school secretary call your mom or dad at work and leave a message.

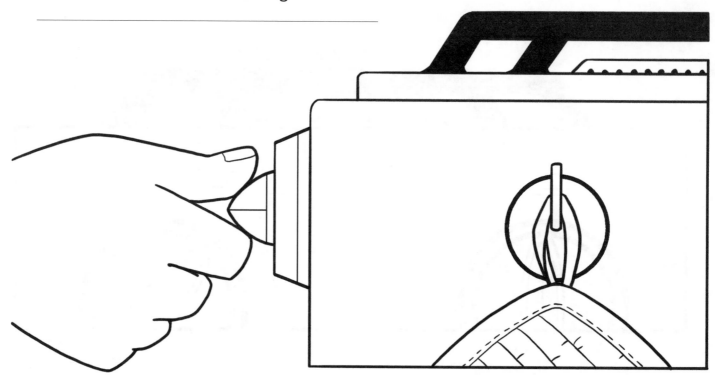

FORGOTTEN **LUNCH**

You get to school and realize that you have forgotten your lunch.

Your folks are at work, and no one else is home. You don't have

enough money with you to buy a meal.

FORGOTTEN **LUNCH**

- Follow your school's policy for receiving an emergency lunch.

- If your school does not have an emergency policy, ask your teacher if you can use your cell phone or go to the school office and ask the secretary if you can call your parents.

- If you can't reach your parents, find a friend who may be willing to share some of his or her lunch with you.

FORGOTTEN **HOMEWORK**

When your teacher calls for homework, you realize that you have

forgotten yours. This is the last day you can turn in the assignment

for credit, but no one can bring it to you today.

- Explain the situation to your teacher. If this is the first time you have forgotten an assignment, he or she may let you bring it tomorrow.

- If you have forgotten to bring your homework before, you may find it helpful to keep a list of assignments and the dates on which they are due in your planner.

- Also, it is easy to forget things when you are in a hurry. Instead of waiting until morning, get your books and papers together on the night before they are due, when you have more time to think, organize, and remember.

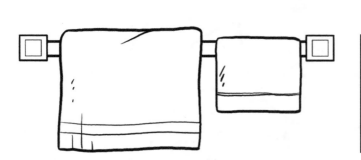

CONFUSED INSTRUCTIONS

While sitting in class, you realize that you are confused about what you are supposed to do after school. You know you are scheduled to go to a book club meeting at the library, but you can't remember whether your mom told you to walk there on your own or wait for her to pick you up.

CONFUSED **INSTRUCTIONS**

- During lunch, go to the school office and talk to the secretary.

- Explain that you are scheduled to go to a book club meeting after school but are uncertain about whether you are supposed to walk or wait for a ride.

- Ask if you can use the phone to call your mom and clarify her instructions.

MENSTRUATION

While in the bathroom at school, you discover

that your menstrual period has started.

You don't have any supplies with you.

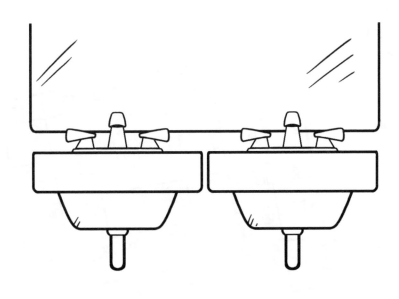
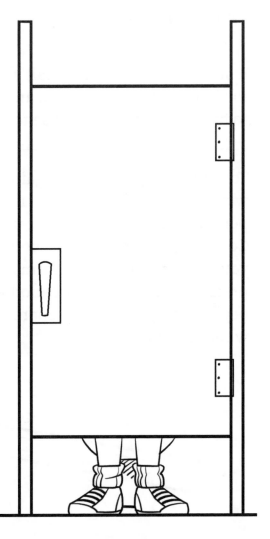

- Ask your teacher if you can be excused from class to go see the school nurse. The nurse will have everything you need.

- If your clothing is soiled, call your mom, explain the problem, and ask her to bring you something else to wear.

- To avoid being surprised again in this way, circle the dates of each menstrual period on a small personal calendar. Count the number of days between your periods. Use this information to predict when your next period will begin and to be better prepared for it when it does.

- For many young women, menstrual cycles are irregular and menstrual periods are difficult to predict. If you are one of these young women, you may want to keep a sanitary napkin in your school locker or carry one in your purse to avoid the inconvenience and possible embarrassment of being caught unprepared.

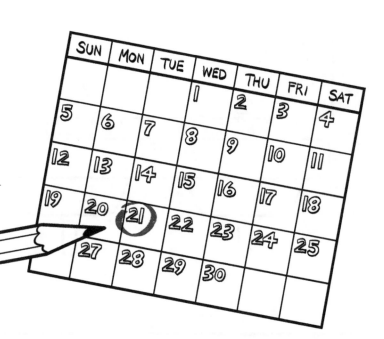

STOLEN **PROPERTY**

When you return from lunch, you find that the 10 baseball cards you brought to school for sharing time are missing from your desk.

- Ask classmates who sit near you if they saw anyone looking in your desk.

- Tell your teacher that the cards are missing. Explain that they are special to you and request that he or she ask class members if they have any idea where the cards might be. Say that you'd like for anyone who finds the missing cards to put them back in your desk, no questions asked.

- The next time you bring an item of value for sharing, ask your teacher to place it in his or her desk for safekeeping until sharing time.

FINDING A
BAG OF PILLS

While at recess, you find a small plastic bag of pills on the school playground.

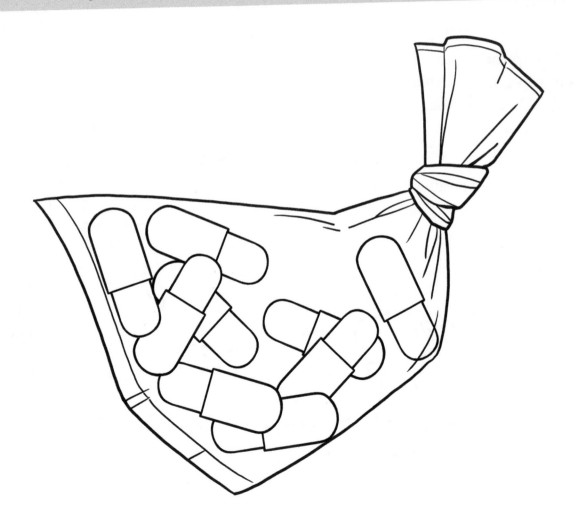

FINDING A **BAG OF PILLS**

- Do not open the bag.

- Do not touch, taste, or swallow any of the pills.

- Do not keep the bag of pills until after class or after school. Take it to your teacher, school secretary, or principal immediately.

- Tell him or her exactly when and where you found the bag.

EMERGENCY **PICKUP**

As you are walking to school alone, a stranger comes up to you and says

that your mother has just been hurt in an automobile

accident. The stranger offers to drive you to the

hospital so you can see your injured mother.

- Do not go with the stranger. He or she probably knows nothing about your mother and has made up the accident story to get you into the car.

- Take a good look at the stranger and the car so that you will be able to tell a police officer or sheriff's deputy what they look like. Pay special attention to the letters and numbers on the license plate.

- Go to the nearest house where adults might be home. Tell the first one you see about the stranger and the car.

- If there is no house nearby where adults are home, join a group of kids and walk with them to school.

- When you get to school, go straight to the office and tell the secretary or principal about the stranger.

- With permission, use the school phone to call your mom and assure yourself that she is really OK.

PARENTS In an emergency, it may be necessary for your child to be picked up by someone he or she has not met or may not recognize. To avoid confusion, decide on a secret password with your child. Caution your child always to ask for that password before accepting a ride from a stranger. And remember to let any emergency driver you authorize in on the secret!

THREATENED

An older kid corners you on the playground

and threatens to beat you up if you don't

give him your lunch money.

- If a teacher or some other adult is within earshot, yell for help.

- If no one is around, ignore the kid. Don't give him your money just because he asks for it. Giving him your money might encourage him to threaten you again.

- If the kid takes your money, go immediately to the school office and report the incident. Tell how much money was taken and describe the kid who took it. In your description, include age or grade, height, weight, color of hair and eyes, and any unusual articles of clothing you may have noticed.

FOLLOWED BY A STRANGER

While walking home from school, you notice that you are being followed by a stranger. Something about him makes you feel very uncomfortable.

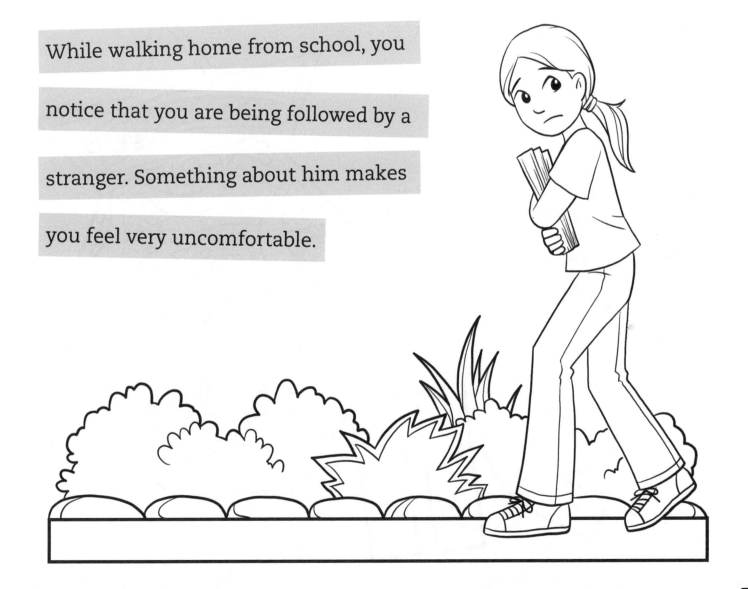

- Look for the nearest house which has signs that an adult is home—an open garage door or kids playing out front.

- Tell the adult that someone is following you and ask him or her to call the police, sheriff's department, or 911.

- Give the officer or deputy a description of the stranger. Include age, height, weight, and color of hair and eyes. Also mention any unusual articles of clothing you may have noticed.

In this section, you will find descriptions of situations you might encounter anywhere when you are out and about. Among these situations are

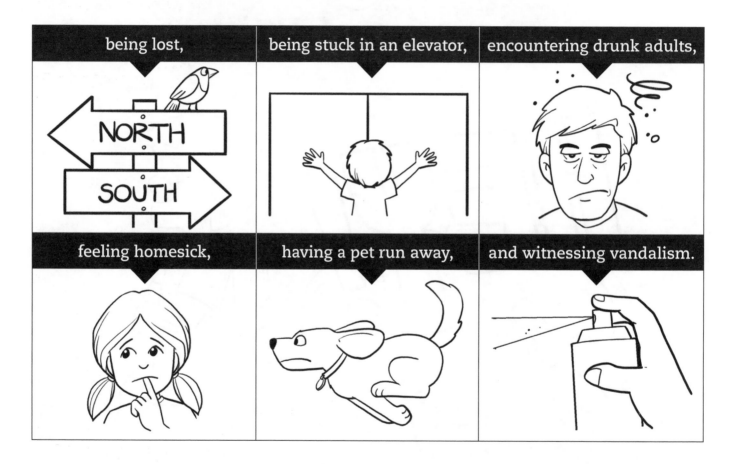

being lost,

being stuck in an elevator,

encountering drunk adults,

feeling homesick,

having a pet run away,

and witnessing vandalism.

First, read about the situation. Next, think about what you would do if you found yourself in this situation. Then, turn the page and read the steps that are listed. Finally, talk over these steps with other members of your family and discuss additional steps you might take in a similar situation.

LOST IN **A STORE**

One afternoon, your dad takes you to the supermarket. Somehow, you become separated from him. Anxiously, you look up and down the aisles, but you can't find him anywhere.

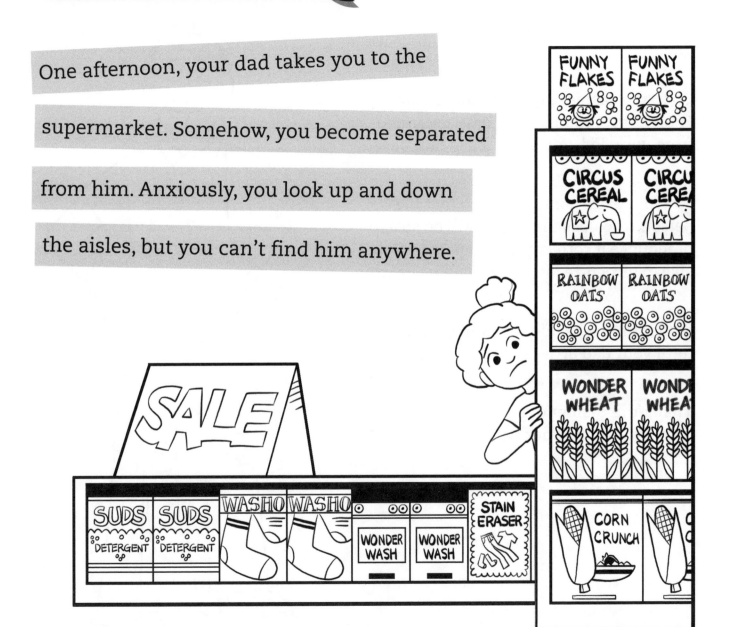

- Stay inside the supermarket. Do not leave.

- Go to the cashier or to the store manager. Explain that you have become separated from your dad, and ask to have him paged.

- Say your dad's name clearly so that the person who does the paging will be able to pronounce it correctly and your dad will be able to recognize his name when he hears it.

- Wait with the cashier or store manager until your dad arrives.

- Thank the cashier or store manager for helping you find your dad.

STUCK IN
AN ELEVATOR

You go to visit your grandparents. While you are riding an elevator to their fifth-floor apartment, it becomes stuck between floors. Much to your dismay, you are alone in the car.

- Wait a minute. Press the **close door** button. Then press the floor button again.

- If the elevator still does not move, press the **emergency button**, which is usually red. An alarm will sound so other people will know that the elevator is stuck.

- If there is no emergency button or no alarm sounds, attract attention by banging on the floor, door, or walls and by shouting loudly for help. Sooner or later, someone will hear the noise and come to your rescue.

LOST **CHILD**

You are shopping with your mother in a busy department store. She asks you to keep an eye on your younger brother while she goes to the restroom. As you are walking with him through the toy department, he suddenly disappears.

- Tell the salesperson right away. He or she will ask store security people to look for your brother.

- To help security people find your brother, tell them how tall he is, what color of hair and eyes he as, and what kind of clothes he is wearing.

- Do not leave the toy department because your mom will expect to find you there when she returns.

BULLY

You are standing in line to buy tickets for a movie. An older kid walks up and asks if he may cut in front of you. When you say no, he calls you names and pushes you around.

- Do not call him names or push him.

- Without saying what you plan to do, leave the line and go to the theater lobby.

- Find a theater employee—a ticket seller, a ticket taker, an usher, or a manager.

- Explain to the theater employee what has happened and describe the person who pushed you.

- If the theater employee does nothing, you can either go to the end of the line or use your cell phone to call home and explain the situation to your parents.

- Next time, bring along a friend or family member. That way, if something similar to this happens again, you are not alone.

FONDLING **STRANGER**

You are sitting in a darkened theater watching a movie. The man in the chair next to yours puts his hand in your lap.

··

- Immediately leave your seat and move to the aisle.

- Even though the theater is dark, try to get a good look at the man.

- Go to the lobby.

- Find an usher or other theater employee and explain what has happened.

- Give the theater employee a description of the man. Include size, age, length and color of hair, type of clothing, and whether the stranger has a beard or mustache.

- If the theater employee does nothing, ask to use the telephone, call home, explain the situation to your parents, make arrangements to leave the theater without seeing the rest of the movie, and demand for a refund of the ticket price!

RUNAWAY **PET**

You are walking your dog when he suddenly sees a cat. Excited,

he dashes after the animal, pulling the leash from your hand.

- Don't dash into the street after your dog.

- Try to get your dog's attention by clapping your hands loudly or whistling.

- Call your dog's name to see if he or she will come back to you.

- If you must follow your dog, stop at the curb, look both ways, and cross the street only when you are certain it is safe to do so.

- If your dog does not respond to your call and you are unable to find the animal, go home and ask one of your parents to drive you back to the place where your pet ran away. Bring along a treat for your dog, and call his or her name as you search.

- If no adult is home at your house, ask a neighbor to help you or call the local animal control office.

CAUTION Animal control officers are often unable to return found pets to their owners because the animals do not carry adequate identification. For your dog's protection, license the animal, place an identification tag on your pet's collar, and make certain that your dog is wearing the collar and tags each time he or she goes outside. You can also take your pet to a veterinarian to be microchipped. This way, if your pet gets lost again, it can be scanned for the microchip that will reveal a unique identification number. That number will be called into the pet recovery service, and you will be contacted using the information in the microchip database.

LOST **RING**

While trying on clothes in a department store, you lose the ring your grandmother gave you. You look in the dressing room and in other places throughout the store, but you can't find it. The ring is not expensive, but it has a lot of sentimental value.

- Go to the store's customer service window, and explain what has happened.

- Leave your name, telephone number, and a description of the ring.

- Tell salespeople in the departments where you shopped about your missing ring. Let them know that you have left your name and telephone number at the customer service window.

LOST RING
- CIRCLE OF GOLD HEARTS
- LOST HERE APRIL 25

Amy Robinson
555-0102
or
555-0198

What Would You Do? © 2018 Creative Teaching Press

DEAD CELL PHONE BATTERY

You are shopping at the mall with a friend and need to make an important phone call. When you take out your cell phone, you realize that the battery has died and you have left your charger at home.

- Do not ask a stranger to borrow their phone.

- Go to the mall information desk or to a store clerk. Explain your situation and ask to use an office or business telephone for your call.

- To avoid this problem in the future, always carry a phone charger or portable power bank.

INJURED **ANIMAL**

While walking with a friend, you notice a cat lying in the street near the curb. When you get closer, you see that the cat's leg is bleeding.

You decide that this poor animal probably has been hit by a car.

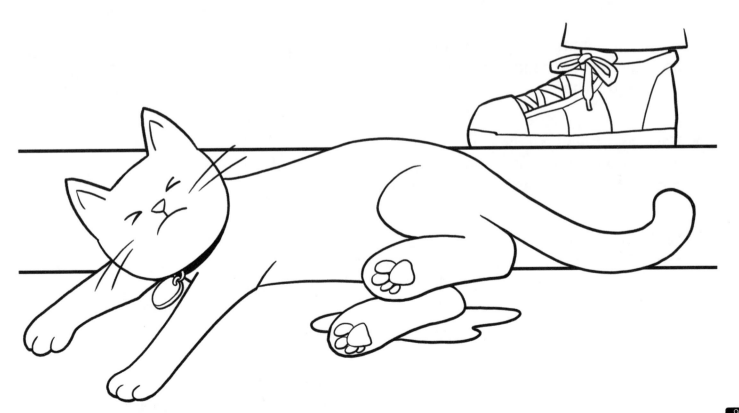

- Do not pet, lift, or try to move the cat. Do not try to give it food or water.

- If you can do so safely, check to see if the cat is wearing an identification tag on its collar.

- If you find a tag, look for the name, address, and/or telephone number of the cat's owner, and ask your friend to contact this person.

- If you cannot find a tag or cannot reach the owner, ask your friend to call animal control officers, the Humane Society, or the police.

- Have your friend tell the person who answers where the cat is and what has happened to it, and ask what you should do.

- While your friend makes the telephone calls, stay with the cat. If the day is unusually hot, shade the injured animal from the sun.

- Without endangering your own life, try to call the attention of approaching motorists to the cat and to wave them away from it.

PET OWNERS Have your cats and dogs wear on their collars identification tags that carry your name and telephone number so that anyone who finds your lost or injured pet will know how to find you!

THUNDERSTORM

One Saturday morning, you decide to meet a friend in the park to play ball. While you are waiting for your friend to arrive, the sky grows dark and is pierced by jagged bolts of lightning. Rain begins to fall. Loud claps of thunder echo all around.

THUNDERSTORM

- Lightning is a powerful discharge of electricity and can be very dangerous. A lightning bolt usually moves from one cloud to another or from a cloud to the ground. It often strikes the highest thing in its path.

- Do not stand under a large tree or take refuge in a metal shed. You will be safer if you remain out in the open, away from things that are tall or are made of metal.

- Keep away from electrical poles and overhead wires because these also can conduct electricity.

AT HOME

- If you are at home during a thunderstorm, stay away from windows, doors, garages, and porches.

- Don't take a bath during a thunderstorm. Many bathtubs are made of coated metal. Both metal and water are good conductors of electricity.

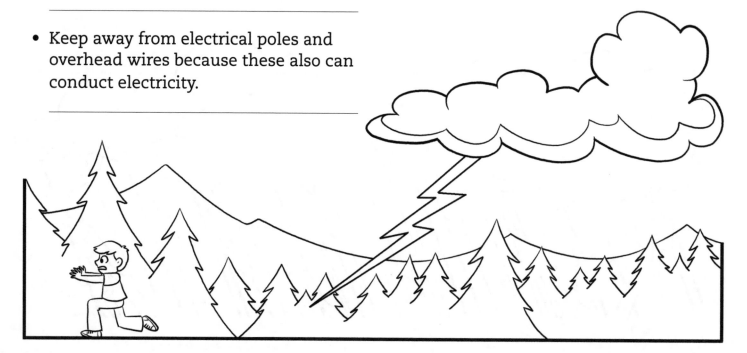

BED-**WETTING**

You are spending the night with a friend and are worried because you sometimes wet the bed at night.

- You are not alone. Many older kids have this problem.

- Avoid drinking fluids at bedtime.

- Go to the bathroom just before you climb into bed.

- Place a bath towel in your bed or sleeping bag to absorb excess moisture.

- When you sleep away from home, take along a change of clothes, just in case.

NOTE Placing a flannel-coated rubber sheet between the mattress pad and the bottom bedsheet when you make the bed will prevent moisture from soaking into the mattress and make middle-of-the-night bedding changes easier.

HOMESICKNESS

You are at a friend's house and had planned to spend the night, but being

away from home no longer seems like a good idea. You don't want to stay,

but you are embarrassed to tell your friend's parents how you feel.

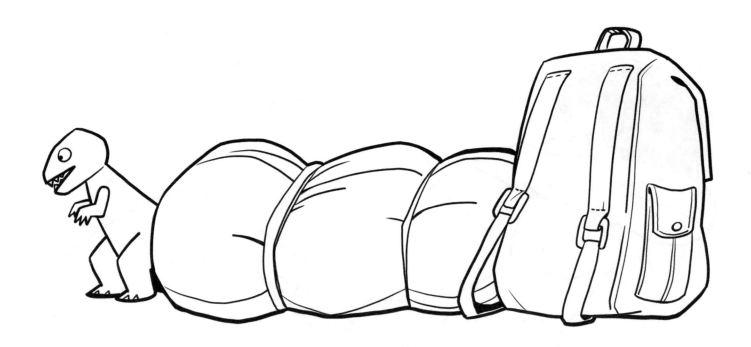

- Many children feel homesick at one time or another, especially when they are sleeping in a strange place or away from home for the first time.

- Don't be embarrassed about the way you feel. Tell your friend's parents. Sometimes, talking about your feelings can make you more comfortable with them.

- If you still want to go home, call your mom or dad and ask one of them to come get you.

- In the future, when you plan to sleep away from home, bring a favorite blanket, stuffed animal, or other possession with you. Familiar objects can make a strange place feel more like home.

DRUNK **ADULTS**

While you are visiting a friend, his parents start arguing loudly and

pushing each other around. The way they are acting makes you feel very

uneasy. You think that they may be drunk, and you want to go home.

- Trust your own feelings. When the situation in one place makes you feel uneasy, uncomfortable, or unsafe, leave that place.

- Call your mom or dad and explain what is happening. If you are concerned that others in the household might overhear your conversation, simply tell your parents that you want to come home. Ask them to pick you up.

- Thank your friend's parents for their hospitality, and then tell them that you have decided to go home and that your parents are coming to pick you up.

- In the future, when you want to spend time with this friend, be the host or hostess rather than the guest. Invite the friend to your house.

VANDALS

While walking your dog early one morning, you notice two older kids

spray-painting words on a neighbor's fence.

When the two see you, they run away.

- Take a good look at the two vandals so that you will be able to give an accurate description of them later. Notice height and weight, color of hair, distinctive items of clothing, and approximate age.

- If the vandals get into a car, notice the make, model, and color of this vehicle and try to remember the letters and numbers on the license plate.

- If you know the people who live in the house, ring their doorbell and tell them what you saw.

- If you do not know the people who live in the house, go directly home and tell your parents what you saw. They will get in touch with the neighbor and/or with the police.

ENAMEL
•SPRAY PAINT•

MIDNIGHT BLACK

A **GUN**

You are playing at a friend's house while her parents are gone. Your

friend shows you where her dad's gun is

hidden. She takes it out and suggests that

the two of you use it to play cowgirls.

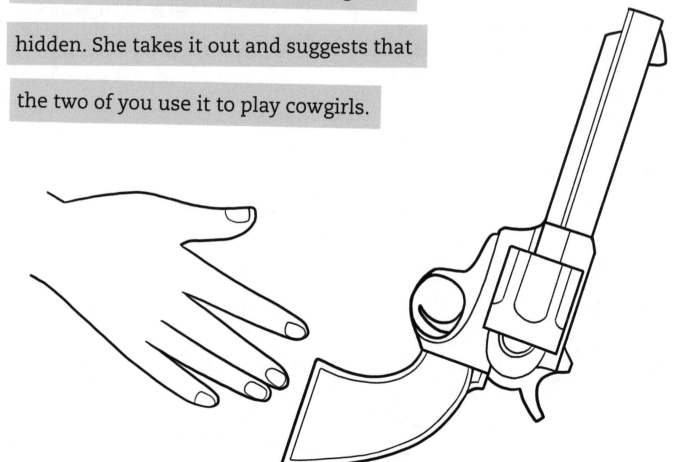

- Guns are weapons, not playthings. They are deadly. Never point a gun at someone else or allow a gun to be pointed at you, even as part of a joke.

- Never pull the trigger thinking that a gun isn't loaded. Assume that any gun you see is both real and loaded, and treat it with extreme caution.

- If a playmate takes out a gun, leave the house immediately.

- Go home and tell your parents about the gun. They will probably suggest to your friend's parents that they find a safer place to store the weapon.

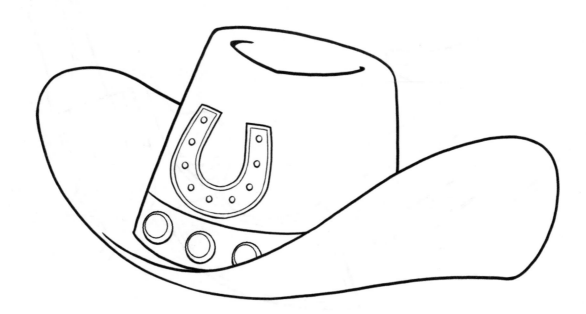

DRUGS

While you are walking to the basketball courts, you meet a group of older kids from your school. One of them offers you drugs.

- Say no and walk away. Don't let anyone bully you into doing something you believe is wrong for you!

- If the older kids approach you again or you feel threatened in any way, report the incident to an adult you trust.

- When you get home, tell your parents what happened.

FIRST AID SITUATIONS

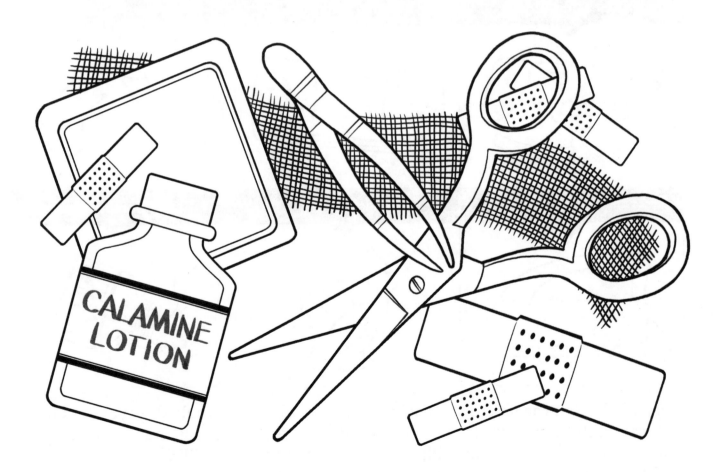

In any emergency, knowledge of basic first aid procedures can make a difference. In major emergencies—such as choking, drowning, and heart attacks—this knowledge can make the difference between life and death. In this section, you will find descriptions of emergency situations you might encounter anytime and anywhere. Among these situations are

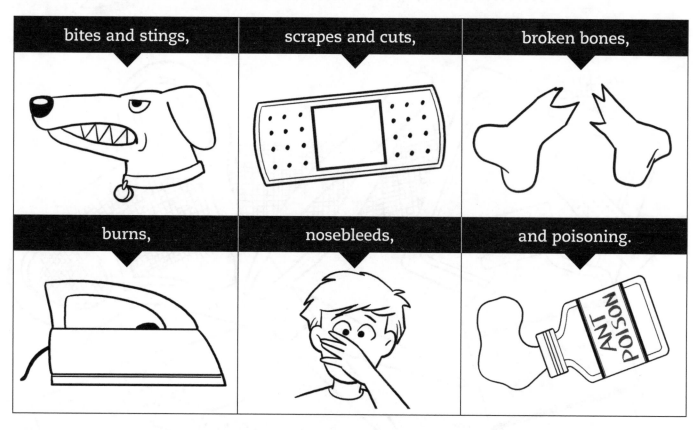

| bites and stings, | scrapes and cuts, | broken bones, |
| burns, | nosebleeds, | and poisoning. |

First, read about the situation. Next, think about what you would do if you found yourself in this situation. Then, turn the page and read the steps that are listed. Finally, talk over these steps with other members of your family and discuss additional steps you might take in a similar situation.

ANIMAL **BITE**

You are playing catch with your new puppy. In her excitement, the dog

bites your hand while trying to get the ball. Your hand starts to bleed.

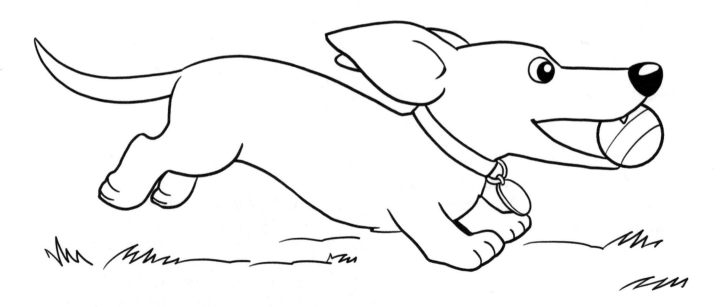

- Tell your parents about the bite so that they can help you with the following steps.

- Wash the bite thoroughly with soap and water.

- Hold a sterile gauze pad firmly on the bite until the bleeding stops.

- Apply an antiseptic to the bite.

- Cover the bite with an adhesive bandage.

- Your parents may want to ask a doctor what additional steps you should take to guard against possible rabies or tetanus infection.

CAUTION ⚠ If you are ever bitten by a stray animal, it is important for someone to call animal control officers immediately so they can catch the animal. They will watch the animal to see if it has rabies and report what they learn to your doctor.

TICK **BITE**

You are camping with your family in a national park. When you return from a morning hike, you discover a tick on your leg.

- Do not try to brush or burn off the tick or to pull it loose.

- Instead, cover the tick with a thick coat of petroleum jelly to close its spiracles, or air holes. Unable to breathe, the tick will suffocate and will probably drop off your leg in less than 30 minutes.

- If the tick does not fall off, remove it with tweezers. Work slowly so that you do not crush the tick or separate the body from the head.

- Once the tick has been removed, wash the area of your leg around the tick bite with soap and water for a full five minutes.

- Apply a topical anesthetic to the bite area to relieve the itching so that you will not be tempted to scratch it.

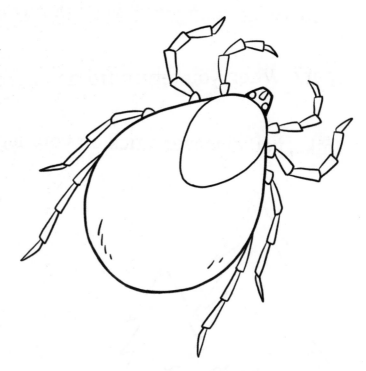

CAUTION

⚠️ Ticks can carry several illnesses, including Lyme disease. Watch the bite area closely. If it becomes swollen and inflamed or if you develop a fever, see a doctor and ask to be tested for Lyme disease.

BEE **STING**

At a public beach, a bee stings you on the arm. The skin around

the sting turns red and begins to swell. It is painful.

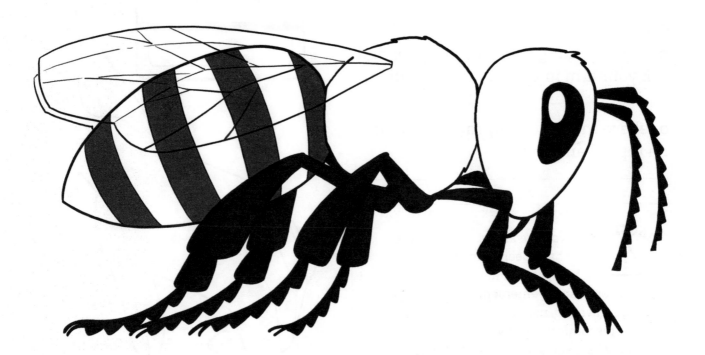

- Remove the stinger if possible.

- Cooling the arm will relieve the pain and slow the absorption of poison. Run cold water over the arm.

- Apply an ice pack if one is available. See page 134.

- When you go home, dissolve a small amount of baking soda in cool water and soak your arm in this soothing solution.

- To relieve the itch, apply calamine lotion or a topical anesthetic.

CAUTION ⚠ If you are allergic to bee stings or have been stung by several bees, go to a lifeguard, first aid station, or hospital emergency room. While you are traveling, use cool compresses to relieve discomfort. After you arrive, you will probably be given some antihistamines to lessen your body's reaction to the stings.

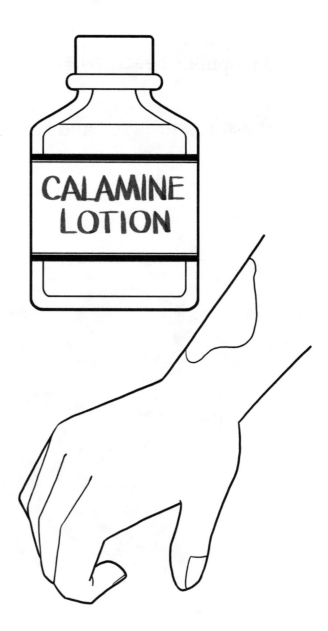

POISON **IVY**

After returning from a picnic with your friend's family, you break out in

a rash. From past experience, you suspect that the cause is poison ivy.

- Wash the rash area thoroughly but gently with soap and water. Do not scrub hard with a cloth or brush.

- Put on calamine lotion to ease the itching.

- When blisters form, do not scratch them. Breaking the blisters and rubbing the fluid they contain on your skin may cause the rash to spread.

CAUTION Learn to watch for, recognize, and avoid poison ivy, oak, and sumac. If you frequently come in contact with one or more of these plants and are seriously bothered by exposure to them, ask your doctor about the possibility of immunization.

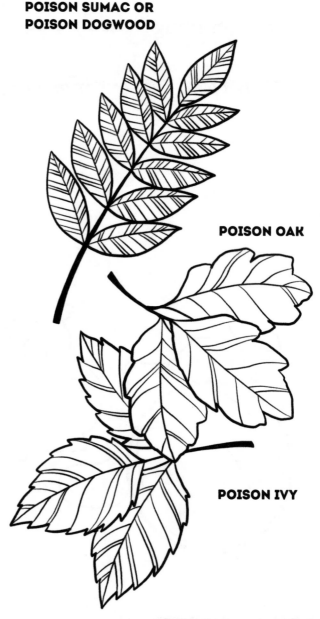

POISON SUMAC OR POISON DOGWOOD

POISON OAK

POISON IVY

SCRAPED **KNEE**

While roller skating in front of your house, you trip, fall, and scrape your knee.

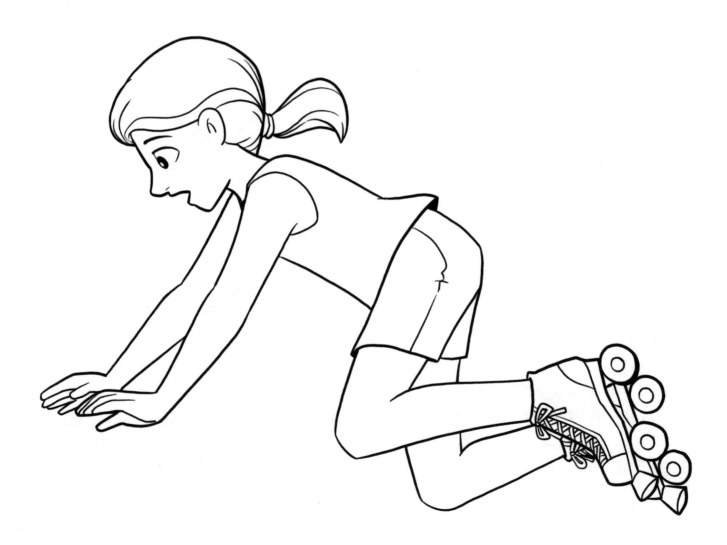

- Wash your hands with soap and water.

  _____

- Using a clean cloth, carefully brush or wipe away any loose dirt or debris that may be on your skin near the scrape.

  _____

- Wash the area around the scrape with soap and water, being careful to rinse away from the wound, not toward it.

  _____

- Gently pat the scraped area dry with a piece of sterile gauze.

  _____

- Apply an antiseptic to the scraped area.

  _____

- When you bandage the scrape, be careful not to put adhesive directly on the wound.

  _____

CAUTION ⚠ When skin is broken, there is the possibility of infection. If the area around the scrape becomes hot, painful, reddened, or swollen, see a doctor at once.

CUT **FINGER**

You are home alone and get hungry. You go into the kitchen

to fix a sandwich. While you are slicing a tomato, the knife

slips and cuts your finger. You can't stop the bleeding.

- Wash the cut finger thoroughly with soap and water.

  _____

- Hold your cut finger under cold running water.

  _____

- Wrap a paper towel or napkin snugly around your finger.

  _____

- Hold your wrapped finger above your head to slow the bleeding.

  _____

- After the bleeding has stopped, apply an antiseptic and a sterile adhesive bandage.

  _____

SPLINTER **IN FINGER**

While sanding a piece of wood for a Scout project, you get a splinter in your finger.

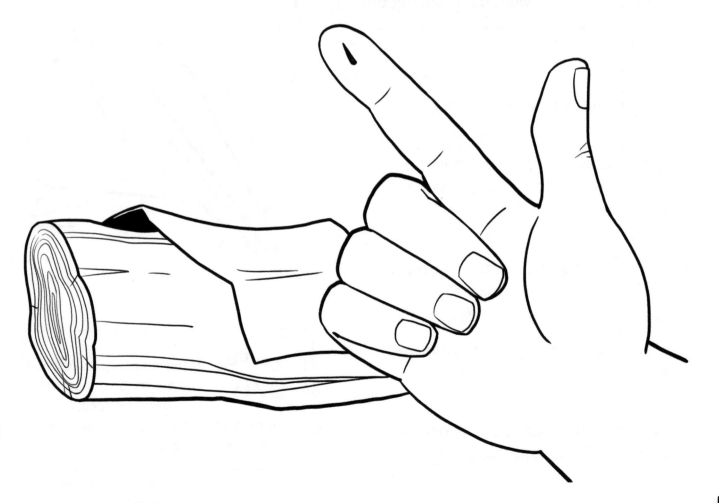

- Wash your hands with soap and water, being especially careful to clean the area around the splinter.

- Sterilize a pair of tweezers by wiping the ends with alcohol, bleach, or hydrogen peroxide.

- Rub ice on the splinter area to numb it.

- Using the sterile tweezers, grab the splinter and pull it out in the same direction as it went in.

- After removing the splinter, squeeze the injured finger to encourage slight bleeding.

- Again, wash the finger with soap and water.

CAUTION If the splinter breaks while you are trying to remove it, is deeply lodged, or is beneath a fingernail, ask an adult for help or see a doctor.

- Apply an antiseptic to the wound, and cover it with an adhesive bandage.

PUNCTURE **WOUND**

While hanging a poster on the wall in your

room, you hammer a nail into your finger.

Although the nail does not go in deeply,

when you pull it out, your finger bleeds.

- Gently squeeze your finger to encourage slight bleeding.

- Wash your hands thoroughly with soap and water.

- Apply an antiseptic to the wound, and cover it loosely with an adhesive bandage.

- Tell your mom or dad what happened. You may need a tetanus booster if you haven't had one in the past five to seven years.

CAUTION If the wound is deep, see a doctor so he or she can protect you from infection by making certain that the wound has been thoroughly cleaned.

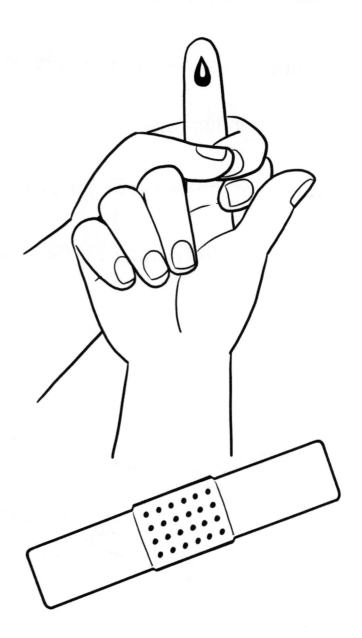

PARTICLE **IN EYE**

While you are playing at the beach, some pesky kid throws

sand at you. Some of the grit lands in your eye.

- Do not rub the eye.

- Look at your eye in a mirror (if one is available). One at a time, gently lift your eyelids to see if the sand is stuck to either of them.

- If the sand is on either lid, try to remove it by touching it lightly with the moistened corner of a clean handkerchief.

- If the sand is not on a lid but is on your eye, don't touch it.

- Cup your hand and fill it with clean water. Use this water to rinse your eye.

- Tell your parents about the sand-throwing incident, and see a doctor as soon as possible.

CHEMICAL **IN EYE**

While you are performing a science experiment with your new chemistry

set, you accidentally splash a chemical mixture into your eye.

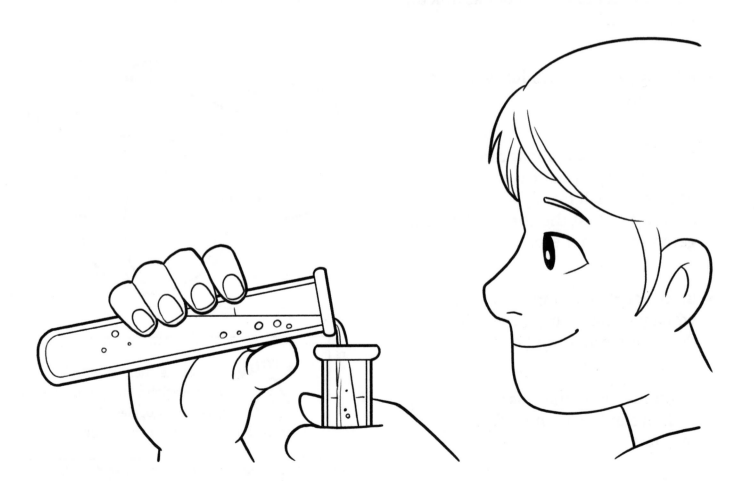

- The stronger the chemical mixture is and the longer it remains in your eye, the greater the harm it may do. For this reason, you want to dilute the chemical mixture as much as possible and to rinse it out as quickly as possible.

- Fill a large glass with lukewarm (not hot) water.

- Holding the glass about three inches from your eye, pour the water into your eye. Flush from your nose outward so that the chemical does not get in your other eye.

- Blink your eye as much as possible while you are pouring water into it, but do not force your eyelid open.

- Continue filling the glass and rinsing your eye in this manner for 15 minutes.

- When your mom or dad comes home, tell him or her what happened.

- Visit a doctor to have the injured eye checked.

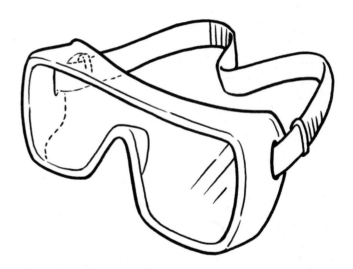

CAUTION Don't take chances with your eyesight. Buy protective glasses or goggles. Wear them each time you work with chemicals.

BLACK **EYE**

Your parents are not home. You are playing

catch with a friend. He throws the ball high

and hard. It strikes you in the eye.

- A black eye is really a bruise. Discoloration of the skin around the eye is caused by the breaking of tiny blood vessels in this area. You don't need to seek medical help for an injury of this kind unless the skin has been cut, the eye itself has been damaged, or facial bones have been broken.

- Do not rub or wash your eye.

- Check to make sure that you have no cuts and no loss of vision.

- To ease the pain and slow the swelling, hold an ice bag or small towel that has been soaked in ice water and wrung out on the eye area.

IMPROVISING AN ICE BAG

If you do not have an ice bag, improvise. Put some ice cubes into a sturdy, watertight plastic bag. Seal the top of the bag. Wrap a washcloth or small towel around the bag. Hold the bag on the injured area. When the ice inside the bag melts, pour out the water and refill the bag with fresh ice.

NOSEBLEED

While roughhousing with your brother, you get hit in the face. Your nose starts to bleed.

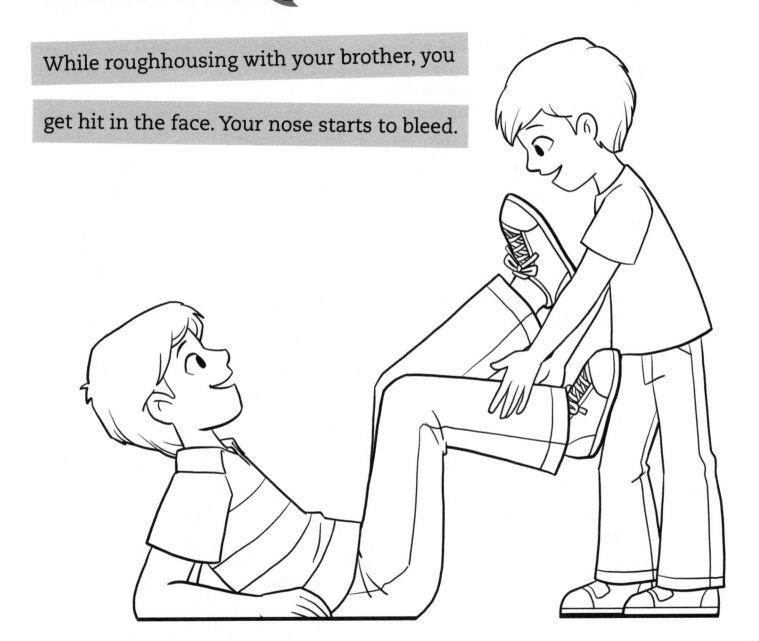

- Sit down on a chair and learn forward, pinching the soft part of your nose together. Remain in this position for 5 to 10 minutes, or until the bleeding stops.

- Placing a folded piece of wet paper towel under your upper lip may help slow the bleeding.

- Laying a cold, damp washcloth or towel across your face may ease the pain and make you feel more comfortable.

TOOTH **KNOCKED OUT**

While playing soccer, you trip and fall, striking your face on the ground.

When you get up, you realize that one

of your front teeth is missing.

- With the help of teammates, search for the missing tooth.

- When you find the tooth, gently rinse it in cool water. Do not use soap or detergent and do not scrub the tooth with a cloth or brush.

- Carefully place the rinsed tooth back into its socket and hold it there.

- If this is not possible, put the tooth into a glass of cool milk or water.

- Get to your dentist as quickly as possible— and don't forget to take your tooth!

HEAD **INJURY**

Your sister falls from a playground swing, hits her head on the ground, and is knocked unconscious.

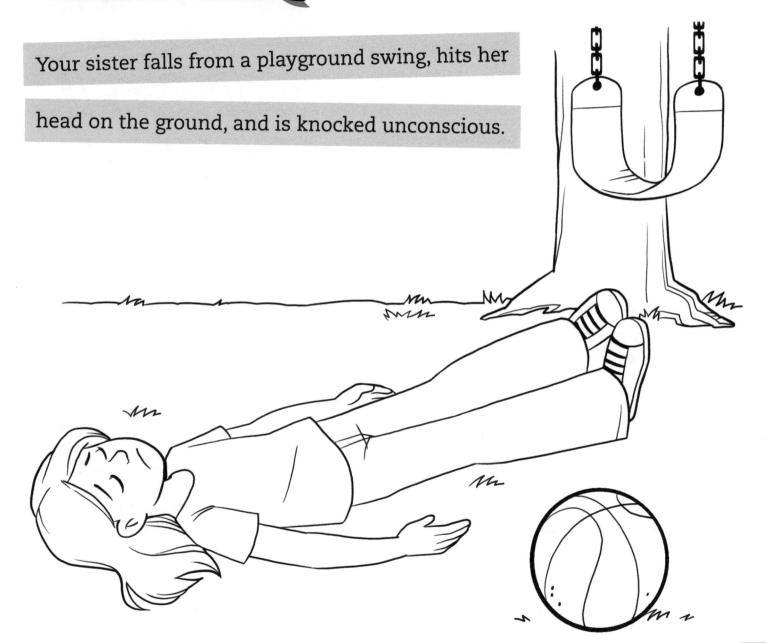

- Ask someone on the playground to call 911.

- Loosen any clothing around your sister's neck if you can do so without moving her.

- Cover her with a blanket, beach towel, or jacket.

- If her head is bleeding, place a sterile bandage or clean folded handkerchief on the wound.

- Gently apply pressure to stop the bleeding if you can do so without moving your sister.

- When your sister regains consciousness, keep her lying down and quite until help arrives.

CAUTION Even if the victim does not lose consciousness, a blow to the head can break blood vessels in the brain, causing it to bleed. For this reason, head injuries should always be taken seriously. If your sister feels dizzy, has headaches, is nauseated, or bleeds from the mouth, nose, or ears, she should be examined thoroughly by a doctor as soon as possible.

BURNED **ARM**

While your older brother is making popcorn, his shirt sleeve catches on fire. You are the only person home with him at the time.

- If your brother runs, rushing air will fan the flames, making the burn worse and possibly spreading the fire. Tell him to drop to the floor and roll his body over his burning arm to smother the flames.

- Turn off the stove.

- Call 911. Tell the operator what has happened, and give your name and address.

- Put a blanket over your brother, but leave his burned arm uncovered.

- Using scissors, carefully cut away clothing from the burned area. If bits of cloth stick to the skin, cut around them; don't try to pull them loose.

- Dip a clean sheet or towel in cold water, squeeze out the excess moisture, and lay the dampened cloth on your brother's injured arm.

- Keep your brother as quiet as possible. Reassure him by telling him that help is on the way.

- Do not bandage the arm or apply medication of any kind. Wait for help to arrive.

INJURED **BACK**

Your grandmother trips and falls down a flight

of stairs. She says that her back and neck hurt.

You are the only person there to help her.

- Tell your grandmother to lie flat. Do not let her try to get up.

- Call 911. Tell the operator what has happened, and give your name and address.

- Loosen any clothing around your grandmother's neck if you can do so without moving her.

- Cover her with a blanket, and make her as comfortable as possible.

- If your house or apartment is hard to find, go outside so that you will be able to direct paramedics to it. If your house is not hard to find, stay with your grandmother and reassure her by telling her that help is on the way.

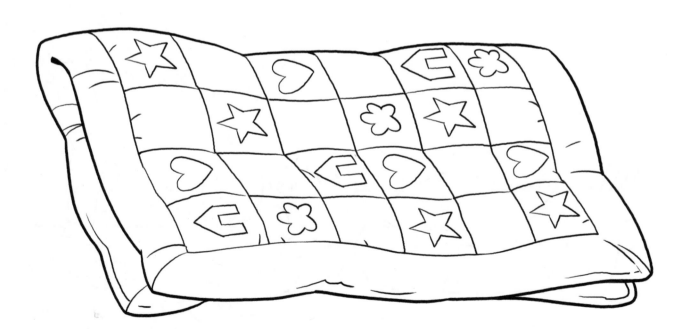

What Would You Do? © 2018 Creative Teaching Press

SPRAINED **ANKLE**

You are skating near your home. Without warning, your right ankle buckles.

You fall to the ground. You feel a throbbing pain in the twisted joint.

- Although your ankle hurts a lot, it is probably not broken.

- As soon as you are able, limp home.

- Improvise an ice bag. See page 134.

- Elevate your injured ankle. Sit with your foot resting on a chair, a footstool, or an ottoman, or lie down and put your foot on a pillow.

- Apply the ice bag to your ankle to reduce pain and lessen swelling.

- Sprains are often slow to heal. During the healing period, avoid putting weight on your injured joint. When you must walk, the weakened ankle will be less painful and less likely to be reinjured if it has the added support of a properly wrapped Ace bandage.

CAUTION It is often impossible to tell the difference between a bad sprain and a break without X-rays. If your ankle continues to hurt even when you are not putting any weight on it, you may have broken a bone in your ankle or foot and should see a doctor.

BROKEN **BONE**

You are playing ball with your younger sister while your parents are away. She trips and falls. When you get to her, she tells you that her arm hurts really bad. You think that the bone might be broken.

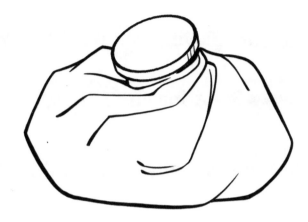

- Have your sister lie down and remain quiet. Cover her with a blanket to keep her warm.

- Do not ask your sister to try to move her arm. Instead, tell her to keep the arm still.

- Apply an ice pack to the injured arm to prevent swelling and ease pain. Do not attempt to splint the arm yourself.

- Once your sister is comfortable, get in touch with your parents. Explain what has happened so that they can arrange to take your sister to a doctor.

- If you can't reach your mom or dad, call a relative, neighbor, or family friend.

- If no one is available, call 911 or an ambulance.

CAUTION

- If a broken bone breaks the skin and there is severe bleeding, stop the bleeding by pressing a clean cloth firmly over the wound.
- Do not attempt to push the bone back in place or to clean the wound.
- If the broken bone is in the neck, back, hip, or pelvis, do not try to move the person. Stop the bleeding, cover the victim with a blanket, and call an ambulance.

SUDDEN **ILLNESS**

One evening you are home alone with your baby brother. Suddenly, he gets fussy and begins to cry. When you pick him up, you notice that he feels hot. You suspect that he is running a fever.

- Do not give your brother any medicine.

- Get in touch with your parents. Tell them how your brother is acting, and ask them what you should do.

- While you wait for your parents to come home, make your brother comfortable. Because he may be thirsty, offer him a drink of cold water or fruit juice.

- Suggest that he lie down but don't force him to.

- Put cool, damp (but not dripping) cloths across his forehead and on his outstretched arms and legs.

CAUTION ⚠️ A higher temperature is one way the human body fights disease. For this reason, a fever usually indicates the presence of an infection. Lowering the body temperature may make a sick person more comfortable, but this relief will be temporary unless something is done to cure the infection that has caused the fever. If the fever continues or if other symptoms develop, your brother should be seen by a doctor.

ASPIRIN **OVERDOSE**

As your favorite television program ends, you realize that your younger

brother has been quiet for an unusually long period of time. When you

check on the little fellow, you find him sitting on the bathroom floor

happily chewing pills of some kind. The baby aspirin bottle beside him

is almost empty. The two of you are home alone.

- Save the aspirin bottle so you can read the label and so you can show it to your parents and to the doctor who treats your brother.

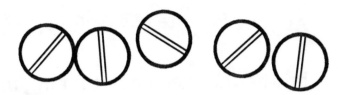

- Call the poison control center or your doctor. Have the aspirin bottle in your hand so you can read the label to the person who answers. Be specific about what your brother has swallowed, and listen carefully to the instructions you are given. Ask questions if you do not understand.

- Try to make your brother gag and spit up the pills he has swallowed by putting your fingers in the back of his throat.

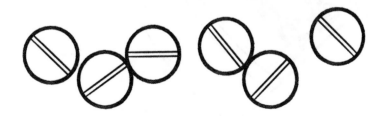

PARENTS Syrup of ipecac is a medicine that causes vomiting. If there are young children in your household, you may want to keep a small bottle of this emetic in your medicine cabinet for emergency treatment of accidental drug overdoses and some other kinds of poisoning.

CAUTION Some common household substances are caustic and can burn mouth, throat, and stomach linings. Among these substances are ammonia, bleach, cleaning fluid, drain opener, lye, paint thinner, toilet bowl cleaner, and turpentine. Never induce vomiting if one of these substances has been swallowed. Doing so may cause additional damage to delicate body tissues.

FAINTING

The startling news that your brother has just won a bike causes him to faint.

- Fainting is a temporary loss of consciousness. It occurs when too little blood flows to the brain. This condition can be caused by an allergic reaction, fatigue, hunger, overexcitement, emotional upset, or a number of other conditions and events.

- Roll your brother onto his back and untangle his arms and legs so that he is lying flat.

- Encourage the flow of blood to your brother's brain by keeping his head low and placing a pillow or rolled-up towel or blanket under his legs to elevate them.

- If the room is stuffy, improve ventilation by opening doors and/or windows.

- To enable your brother to get more air, loosen any tight clothing, including his belt, waistband, or tie.

- To make your brother more comfortable, dip a washcloth in ice water, squeeze the cloth to remove excess moisture, and lay it across your brother's forehead.

- If your brother does not regain consciousness within two minutes, dial 911 and get medical help.

CAUTION

If your brother feels faint but does not lose consciousness, have him sit down on a chair, place his feet firmly on the floor about 6 to 12 inches apart, bend forward until his head is between his knees, and remain in this position until he feels better. To speed his recovery, loosen any tight clothing and increase room ventilation.

HEART **ATTACK**

You and your dad are home alone. Suddenly, he feels pains in the center

of his chest and is short of breath. You

think that he is having a heart attack.

- Help your dad sit or lie down. If he is having difficulty breathing, he may be more comfortable in an upright position.

- If your dad has had heart pains before and has been given some medicine to take, find these pills for him. You may need to take the pills out of their container and to bring your dad a glass of water so that he can take them more easily.

- Call 911, describe the situation and symptoms, and give your complete address.

- Assure your dad that help is on the way.

- Call your mom and tell her what has happened.

- While you are waiting for help to arrive, remain calm and make your dad as comfortable as possible.

- Loosen any tight clothing your dad may be wearing, including his belt, waistband, and tie.

- If your dad is sweating, use a soft washcloth to wipe the excess moisture from his face and neck.

- Hold your dad's hand and talk to him in a reassuring voice.

Your friend is eating peanuts at your house. When a nut gets caught in her throat, she begins to choke.

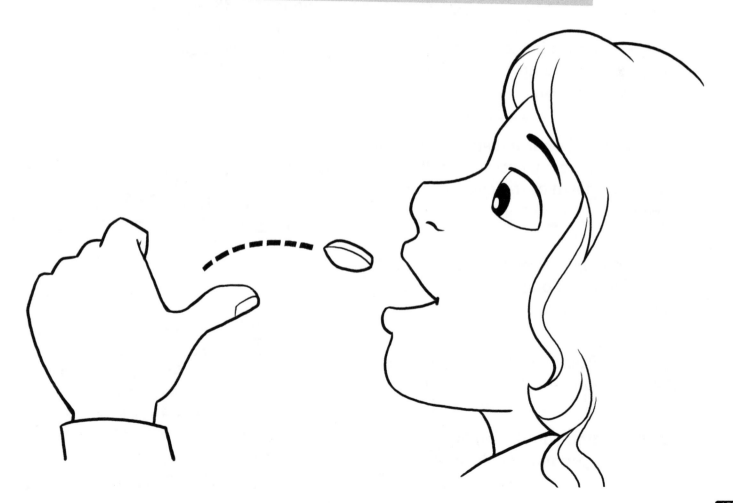

- When the windpipe is blocked, a person cannot speak and will remain conscious for only a few minutes. You need to ask yes-or-no questions, which can be answered by a nod or shake of the head, and you need to act quickly.

- Ask your friend if she can talk. If she shakes her head no, her windpipe is probably blocked.

- If your friend's natural efforts to cough up the nut are unsuccessful, tell her to lie facedown over a chair with her head lower than her body.

- If this change of position does not help your friend dislodge the nut, follow these simple steps.

- Tell your friend to sit in a straight-backed chair.

- Stand behind your friend and bring your arms around her chest.

- Make a fist with one hand and cover the fist with your other hand.

- By pulling on your one fist with your other hand, apply pressure just above your friend's belly button to force air up through the closed windpipe, thereby dislodging the peanut. See page 174.

> **NOTE** After a choking incident of this kind, the victim is likely to feel light-headed and/or slightly nauseated because of the temporary loss of oxygen. Do not be surprised if your friend wants to sit quietly for a while—until she feels better.

DROWNING

You are playing with your friend near a pool. Suddenly, you notice that his younger sister, who cannot swim, has fallen into the deep end of the swimming pool.

- Tell your friend to get help.

- If you know how to swim, jump into the pool and help pull the girl to safety.

- If the girl is near the side of the pool, lie down and extend your arm toward her. Brace yourself so that you will not be pulled in. Tell her to take hold of your hand. When she does so, pull her gently to safety.

- If you cannot reach the girl, hold out a stick, pole, or towel. Brace yourself so that you will not be pulled in. Tell the girl to take hold of this object. When she does so, pull her gently to safety. Avoid jerky motions because a sudden tug may pull the stick, pole, or towel from the girl's grasp.

- If this does not work, throw a cushion, board, or life preserver to the girl. Tell her to take hold of it and kick her way to you.

EARTHQUAKE

You are playing a computer game while your parents are at work.

Suddenly, everything starts to shake. You realize that you are

experiencing an earthquake.

- To avoid being hit by broken glass and falling objects, stay away from windows, bookcases, and shelves.

- Get under a sturdy desk or table, or stand in a doorway.

- After the shaking stops, turn on your radio or television set and listen for news broadcasts.

- When you check for damage, wear shoes to protect your feet from broken glass and open closet cabinet doors carefully.

- Do not use the telephone except to call your parents or to call for help.

- Brace yourself for aftershocks.

- Know how and where to turn off the gas, water, and electricity if necessary. See page 175.

BE PREPARED See page 173 for a list of equipment and supplies you should keep on hand for use after an earthquake or during other similar emergencies.

HURRICANE

You and your family have been warned that a hurricane is expected to hit your community within a few hours.

- If you live in a low, exposed coastal area, shut off your gas, pull your main electrical switch, and leave for a safer place.

- If you plan to stay in your home, be prepared. Collect and put away all loose outside objects, such as trash cans and patio furniture.

- Close and latch shutters. Nail sheets of plywood over exposed windows.

- Check and replenish your food, first aid, and emergency supplies. Fill containers with fresh water. Have flashlight and batteries or candles and matches handy in case the electrical power goes out.

- Listen to your radio for weather updates.

- In a hurricane, the wind and rain stop as the eye, or center, of the storm passes over. Don't be deceived by this temporary calm. Stay inside and away from windows until word is given by the National Weather Service that the storm is over.

AFTER THE STORM

- Listen for bulletins on your radio.

- When you go outside, watch for weakened trees and structures that might fall, and do not touch fallen or low-hanging wires.

LISTS AND CHECKLISTS

In this section, you will find a collection of practical lists and checklists to help you prepare for minor emergencies, avoid major ones, and deal effectively with either. These lists include

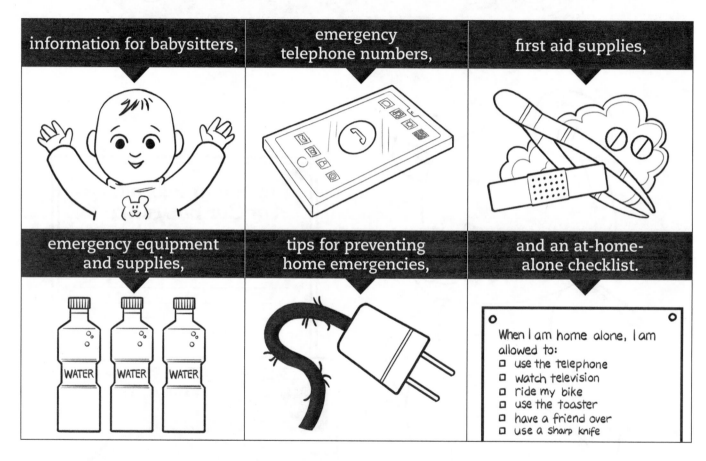

| information for babysitters, | emergency telephone numbers, | first aid supplies, |
| emergency equipment and supplies, | tips for preventing home emergencies, | and an at-home-alone checklist. |

When I am home alone, I am allowed to:
- ☐ use the telephone
- ☐ watch television
- ☐ ride my bike
- ☐ use the toaster
- ☐ have a friend over
- ☐ use a sharp knife

Place these lists on the refrigerator, near the telephone, inside the medicine cabinet, and in other places where they can be easily seen and conveniently used. Refer to them often, update them as needed, and revise them in any way that will make them more useful to you and your family.

FOR _____

When I am home alone, I am allowed to	YES	NO
use the telephone		
have a friend over		
cross the street		
play at a friend's house		
go to the school playground		
ride my bike to a neighbor's house		
fix a snack using a sharp knife		
use the electric can opener		
use the toaster		
use the microwave oven		
use the stove		
use the convection oven		

use these other appliances

_____

_____

_____

Additional Notes:

_____

_____

_____

PARENTS The responsibility you allow your children to take will vary with their ages and maturity levels. Photocopy this page so that you will be able to create a customized At-Home-Alone Checklist for each school-aged child in your family.

EMERGENCY
TELEPHONE NUMBERS

Instructions: Photocopy this page, write in names and/or telephone numbers, and photocopy again so that you will have enough copies to place one next to your home wall calendar and give one to each child to carry in a backpack, billfold, pocket, or purse. Don't forget to update the list as needed.

Emergency   **911**

Fire Department _____

Police or Sheriff's Department _____

Poison Center _____

Family Doctor _____

Ambulance _____

Mother at Work _____

Father at Work _____

Grandparent or Other Relative _____

Neighbor _____

Close Friend _____

Gas Company _____

Electric Power Company _____

Plumber _____

Electrician _____

Veterinarian _____

Other: _____ _____

_____ 'S FRIENDS

Child's Name	Parents' Names	Phone Number
_____	_____	_____
_____	_____	_____
_____	_____	_____

_____ 'S FRIENDS

Child's Name	Parents' Names	Phone Number
_____	_____	_____
_____	_____	_____
_____	_____	_____

_____ 'S FRIENDS

Child's Name	Parents' Names	Phone Number
_____	_____	_____
_____	_____	_____
_____	_____	_____

IMPORTANT INFORMATION
FOR OUR BABYSITTER

Our children's names, ages, and bedtimes are

Name _____ **Age** _____ **Bedtime** _____

Name _____ **Age** _____ **Bedtime** _____

Name _____ **Age** _____ **Bedtime** _____

Our home address is _____

_____

The nearest cross streets are _____

_____

Our home telephone number is _____

We expect to be home around _____

We can be reached at _____

If we can't be reached, you can call

Name _____ **Phone** _____

Our doctor is

Name _____ **Phone** _____

A relative you can call is

Name _____ **Relationship** _____ **Phone** _____

Special Instructions: _____

CHECKLIST OF
FIRST AID SUPPLIES

- [ ] adhesive bandages in assorted sizes and shapes

- [ ] roll of adhesive tape, 1" wide

- [ ] sterile gauze pads, 4" x 4"

- [ ] roll of gauze bandage, 2" wide

- [ ] antiseptic liquid or cream for treatment of minor cuts and scrapes

- [ ] first aid cream or topical anesthetic for relief of itch and pain

- [ ] antibacterial soap

- [ ] baking soda

- [ ] calamine lotion

- [ ] ipecac syrup

- [ ] petroleum jelly

- [ ] hot water bottle

- [ ] ice bag or ice pack

- [ ] packet of needles

- [ ] pair of scissors

- [ ] pair of tweezers

- [ ] oral thermometer

- [ ] rectal thermometer

- [ ] medicine dropper (eyedropper)

- [ ] teaspoon for measuring

EMERGENCY PREVENTION
CHECKLIST

☐ Post emergency telephone numbers in easy view in a central location.

☐ Install smoke alarms on each floor of your house and in all sleeping areas.

☐ Test smoke alarms frequently to be certain that they are in good working order.

☐ Replace smoke alarm batteries regularly.

☐ Check all electrical outlets for smoke or scorch marks, evidence of a faulty connection and possible short.

☐ Replace wires and wall sockets as needed.

☐ Put covers on electrical outlets that are not in use.

☐ Quickly replace all burned-out lightbulbs.

☐ Remove and replace frayed electrical appliance cords.

☐ Cover stove burners and control knobs with protective shields.

☐ Keep toilet seats and lids down. Install seat locks if necessary.

☐ Store medicines, household cleansers, and other caustic and/or potentially poisonous substances beyond the reach of small children.

☐ Install sturdy railings beside all stairs and check regularly to be sure that they provide reliable support.

☐ Use safety gates to block access to stairway entrances.

☐ Repair or replace hall and area rugs that slip and slide.

CHECKLIST OF EMERGENCY EQUIPMENT AND SUPPLIES

☐ batteries

☐ blankets

☐ can opener, manual

☐ fire extinguisher

☐ first aid supplies (see list on page 171)

☐ flashlight

☐ food, canned or dehydrated, to last for several days

☐ gloves, heavy

☐ knife, pocket

☐ lantern, propane

☐ matches

☐ radio, battery-powered or hand-crank weather radio

☐ tools—axe, broom, hammer, screwdriver, and shovel

☐ watch or clock

☐ water, bottled

☐ wrench, crescent

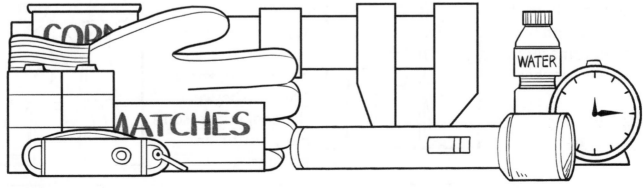

To check for a heartbeat:

Place your index and middle fingers on the side of an unconscious person's neck, slightly below and forward from the base of the jaw.

To stop severe bleeding from an arm or leg:

Hold a sterile gauze pad or folded clean handkerchief on the wound and apply firm, steady, direct pressure for 5 to 15 minutes.

To help a person who is choking:

Tell the person to sit in a straight-backed chair.

Stand behind the person and bring your arms around his or her chest.

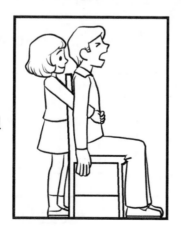

Make a fist with one hand and cover the fist with your other hand.

While pulling on your fist with your other hand, apply pressure between the choking person's belly button and rib cage.

To shut off the gas:

Find the gas shutoff valve located on the gas inlet pipe next to the meter.

Grip the end of the valve firmly with a crescent wrench.

Give it a quarter turn in either direction, from the vertical (ON) position to the horizontal (OFF) position.

Doing so closes the pipe and stops the flow of gas.

To shut off the water:

Locate a water shutoff wheel or the main water valve.

Turn this wheel to the right (clockwise) until the water stops flowing.

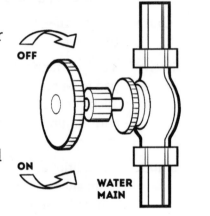

OFF

ON

WATER MAIN

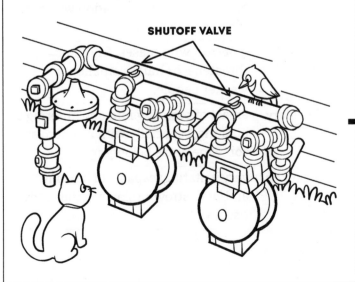

SHUTOFF VALVE

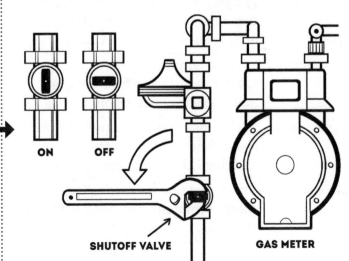

ON   **OFF**

SHUTOFF VALVE   **GAS METER**

GLOSSARY

abrasion   a wound that occurs when the skin is rubbed with something rough so that layers of skin are scraped away.

abuse   rough, cruel, harmful, or inappropriate treatment.

adhesive bandage   a strip of fabric that consists of a gauze pad to be placed over a wound and sticky portions that will adhere to the surrounding skin and hold the pad in place.

aftershock   an additional shake that follows the main shake of an earthquake and is caused by or related to it.

allergic reaction   a symptom or combination of symptoms—such as itching, skin rash, sneezing, swelling, and breathing difficulties—caused by an allergy.

allergy   an unusual sensitivity to a particular substance, such as a fiber, food, hair, mold, pollen, or bee venom.

anesthetic   a substance that causes partial or total loss of feeling, thereby preventing or relieving itch and/or pain.

antihistamine   a medicine that helps to relieve allergy symptoms and control allergic reactions.

antiseptic   a substance that kills and/or prevents the growth and multiplication of infection-causing organisms. Alcohol, boric acid, hydrogen peroxide, iodine, and mercurochrome are common antiseptics.

appliance   an instrument or machine designed for a particular purpose. Can openers, toasters, and washing machines are appliances.

blackout   a period of darkness in a block, district, or city caused when lights go out as the result of a failure of electric power.

bruise   an injury to the body, caused by a fall or blow, that breaks blood vessels and results in discoloration without breaking the skin.

bully   a person who teases, frightens, threatens, or harms smaller or weaker people.

burglary   an act of breaking into and entering a building, especially with intent to steal someone else's belongings.

caustic   very irritating; capable of burning and/or destroying skin or other body tissues.

choke to stop normal breathing by blocking the windpipe or constricting the throat.

circuit breaker a switch that automatically interrupts the flow of electricity in an electric circuit when the current becomes too strong.

concussion an injury to the brain caused by a hard blow to the head. The symptoms of concussions include dizziness, headaches, nausea, and bleeding from the mouth, nose, and/or ears.

conscious awake; aware; able to feel and think; having mental faculties undulled by sleep or faintness.

credit the ability to purchase goods or services now and pay for them later because of established goodwill or reputation of trustworthiness.

cut a wound made by something sharp; gash.

dilute to make weaker or thinner by adding water or some other liquid.

dose the measured amount of a drug or medicine that is supposed to be taken at any one time.

drown to die under water or some other liquid because of lack of air to breathe.

drug any substance that affects the structure of the body and/or changes the way it works.

drunk overcome by the effects of an alcoholic beverage; strongly affected by alcohol; intoxicated.

earthquake a shaking of a portion of the earth's crust caused by the movement of masses of rock along fault lines or by volcanic activity.

emergency an unforeseen combination of circumstances that creates the sudden and unexpected need for immediate action; a serious and potentially life-threatening situation requiring immediate action.

emetic a medicine that causes vomiting. Ipecac syrup is an emetic.

extortion the act of using threats or force to obtain money.

fainting a temporary loss of consciousness that occurs when too little blood flows to the brain. Fainting can be caused by an allergic reaction, fatigue, hunger, overexcitement, emotional upset, or other factors.

fever   an unhealthy condition in which the body temperature is higher than normal (98.6° F). Because a higher temperature is one way that the human body fights disease, a fever is one symptom of illness or infection.

first aid   emergency care or treatment given to a sick or injured person before a doctor comes or other medical help can be obtained.

fondle   to touch, handle, or caress.

fracture   a breaking of bone or cartilage.

fuse   an electrical safety device that consists of fusible metal that melts and interrupts a circuit when the current becomes too strong.

heart attack   an acute cramping of the heart muscle caused by an inadequate flow of blood through coronary arteries.

Heimlich maneuver   a procedure designed to use the air in a conscious choking person's own lungs to dislodge the object that is blocking his or her windpipe. To perform this maneuver, wrap your arms around the choking person's middle just above the navel. Clasping your hands together, press in and up in quick thrusts.

homesickness   a strong and persistent feeling of sadness caused by being far away from home; a strong desire to return home.

hurricane   a storm of tropical origin that has winds that blow at speeds of at least 74 miles per hour and usually brings with it very heavy rain.

illness   an unhealthy condition of body or mind; disease; sickness.

infection   disease caused by small organisms, such as bacteria, fungi, or viruses. Symptoms of infection include fever, pain, and swelling.

lightning   a flash of light in the sky caused by a discharge of electricity between one cloud and another or between a cloud and the ground.

menstruation   a discharge of blood from the uterus that occurs normally in adult women about every four weeks and lasts for several days.

natural gas   a combustible gas formed by decaying material in the earth and used as fuel.

911   the telephone number to dial in a life-threatening emergency that requires immediate aid from fire and rescue teams, the police or sheriff's department, and/or paramedic and ambulance services. For nonemergency calls to these agencies, use the seven-digit numbers listed in the front of your telephone directory or on their websites.

overdose	too large an amount of a drug or medicine taken at one time; the correct amount of a drug or medicine taken too often.
paramedic	one who is trained to give first aid and to assist a physician in providing emergency care or treatment to seriously ill or severely injured persons.
particle	a small fragment as of dust or sand.
password	a secret word or phrase that must be spoken by a person before he or she is allowed to pass a guard or to enter a door or gate; a secret word or phrase used to identify a person as a friend or member.
period	the time during which a girl or women menstruates.
pesticide	a poisonous substance that is used to kill pests, such as insects, rodents, or weeds.
poison	any substance that kills, injures, or impairs a living organism through chemical action.
power outage	an interruption in the flow of electricity to a block, district, or entire city; a blackout.
prowler	someone who goes about secretly searching for something to steal.

puncture	a hole made by something pointed; a deep opening made by a pointed object.
puncture wound	the type of injury made by a long, pointed object, such as a nail.
rabies	a usually fatal virus disease that is transmitted by the bite of infected animals and attacks the central nervous system, causing mental disturbance, muscular spasms, and paralysis.
sanitary napkin	a disposable absorbent pad worn during menstruation to absorb blood discharged from the uterus.
scrape	a superficial wound made when an area of skin is rubbed against something rough; abrasion.
sexual abuse	the inappropriate and unwelcome touching of a private part of a person's body by someone else.
sprain	an injury to a joint caused by a sudden or violent twist that results in the stretching or tearing of ligaments.
sterile	free from infection- or disease-causing organisms.
stranger	any person who is unknown to you; any person you have not previously seen, heard of, or been introduced to.

suspicious causing one to suspect; causing one to feel or believe that a person is not trustworthy, a particular behavior is threatening, and/or a situation is unsafe.

symptom a noticeable change in the normal working of the body that indicates or accompanies the presence of disease, illness, or infection.

tetanus an often-fatal disease that enters the body through a wound, causes violent muscle spasms and stiffness, and can be prevented by inoculation; lockjaw.

thunderstorm a storm with thunder and lightning.

tick a tiny eight-legged relative of the spider that attaches itself to humans and animals, sucks their blood, and may carry disease.

topical anesthetic a substance that is applied to the skin to lessen feeling and, thereby, to relieve itching and/or pain.

unconscious asleep; unaware; unable to feel and think; having mental faculties dulled by faintness or sleep.

vandal a person who defaces, damages, or destroys on purpose objects or property belonging to someone else.

venom poisonous substance secreted by some snakes, spiders, and insects when they bite or sting.

ventilation the act, process, or means of supplying fresh air to a room, building, or other enclosed area.

veterinarian a doctor who specializes in treating animals.

wound an injury caused by hitting, cutting, scraping, stabbing, or tearing in which skin is broken, body tissues are damaged, and some bleeding occurs.

X-ray an electromagnetic ray having an extremely short wavelength which can go through substances that ordinary rays of light cannot penetrate. Photographs made by means of X-rays are used to locate broken bones and to diagnose and treat certain diseases.

INDEX